Helen Gougeon's

Original Canadian Cookbook

Tundra Books
Montreal

Collins Publishers
Toronto

Old Quebec Maple Sugar House

Helen Gougeon's

Original Canadian Cookbook

Illustrated by
Carlo Italiano

For Joseph Schull and Christiane and Joey who like my cooking and Michael who likes hot dogs.

Original edition Copyrighted in Canada, 1958, by the Macmillan Company of Canada under the title *Helen Gougeon's Good Food*

New material © Helen Gougeon Schull, 1975
Cover and illustrations by Carlo Italiano

ISBN 0 00 211598/0

Published in Canada by
Tundra Books of Montreal
Montreal, Quebec H3A 1G3
Legal deposit, Third quarter
Quebec National Library

Published in the United States by
Tundra Books of Northern New York
Plattsburgh, New York 12901
Library of Congress Card No. 75-30482

Printed in Canada

Foreword

This book was compiled in the 50s from recipes that I had
collected all across Canada and published in my column when
I was food editor of *Weekend* Magazine. When it came out,
I was on my way with my husband to spend a year in London,
England. Since then, I've had three children, am still married
to the same husband and have moved to a large old house up
the street from the one where I'd tested all these recipes. I am
now writing a cooking column for *The Canadian* Magazine,
interviewing Montreal's great chefs on a weekly TV show and
helping to run a specialty kitchen shop which a newspaper
confrère, Deirdre O'Connell, and I opened seven years ago.

This paperback edition is much the same as the original book —
it was called simply *Good Food* — which has been out of print
for many years, but I could not resist adding a few new recipes
and I had to up-date a few of the chapter openings.   The
recipes were written for cooks in every large city and many
small towns across Canada — local newspapers included the
magazine in their Saturday editions — so the recipes had to be
practical.   Ingredients had to be found in local shops and they
certainly had to be economical.   A few spices and herbs mentioned here and there might have been exotic in those days
but have become commonplace now. In all, I think as I read
the recipes, they've stood the test of time.   My thanks to May
Ebbitt Cutler of Tundra Books, who thought the recipes had
survived too — she tells me this is the first time she has re-
printed a book originally published by another company.

When I looked closely at the book again, I realized how my thinking — and, indeed, everyone's — has changed since the early 50s. I laughed out loud at a chapter headed "Gentlemen Prefer" in which I talk of "exerting wiles more effectively at the stove ...." Nowadays, men cook for women some of the time and in our kitchen shop, at least half of our customers are male.

In Canada, we have grown up with recipes that the first French and English settlers created and blended together. I remember 25 years ago travelling across Canada and being asked in the West for the "real" recipe for tourtière. Nowadays, the uniquely Quebec pork pie is made everywhere. I know, too, that plum pudding is a must at Christmas among French-speaking Canadians for I sell moulds to hundreds of customers who no longer look on it as a peculiarity of "les Anglais." Other ethnic groups have brought their distinctive recipes from Europe and Asia and adapted them to Canadian ingredients. We have learned to like all these dishes and they seem to be on our table for good. We've come a long way gastronomically and I find people eager to try new utensils and concepts. And they are also going back with enthusiasm to some of the old ways — making bread, ice cream, soup, yogurt, preserves, growing their own vegetables, fruits and herbs.

When *Good Food* was in preparation, I asked a dear friend and colleague, Carlo Italiano, to illustrate it. He did with his usual enthusiasm and generosity. Since that time, Carlo has got a little of the recognition his talents deserve: in 1975 his "Sleighs of My Childhood" was chosen Best Illustrated Book of the Year by the Canadian Association of Children's Librarians. Just as I couldn't resist adding a few new recipes, so Carlo wouldn't hear of the book being republished without adding more drawings — 62 new ones to make a total of 114!

To all the readers and customers who kept asking when my book would be back in print, I am happy to say "Le Voilà."

Rosemere, Quebec, 1975   Helen Gougeon Schull

Contents

Six Canadian Menus

THE RÉVEILLON

When I was a kid I thought that French Canadians celebrated
New Years with parties but observed Christmas Day quietly
as a religious feast. When I was old enough to take part, I
realized the Réveillon, that gay family gathering which started
after Midnight Mass and lasted till dawn, left everyone too
exhausted to lift a turkey into the oven, hence the absence of
Christmas Dinner, as we knew it, in French-speaking homes.

In our household which was French-Irish, we had all the
traditions, a Réveillon *and* a Christmas Dinner, usually with
lots of relatives and friends at both. My mother remembers
one Christmas when she prepared a Réveillon, put a turkey
in the oven as she was going to bed, got up to serve dinner to
our own family at two p.m. and then went out Christmas night
with my father to a grown-up family dinner at Aunt Nellie's.
"Those were the days," she says today rather wistfully.
Saner eating habits have edited the menu drastically since the
old days, and this is what I would call a pared-down Réveillon
for the 70s.

> **Pickled Eggs**
> **Tourtière**
> **My Best Fruit Chili**
> **Hors d'Oeuvre Turnips**
> **Doughnuts**
> **Christmas Cake**
> **Coffee (lots of it)**

NEW YEAR'S EVE

There are two kinds of New Year's Eves in my memory. I remember an intimate one at Jehane and Bernard Benoit's home in Montreal before they moved to the Eastern Townships to raise sheep. The menu was unusual — and exquisite: champagne, artichoke hearts in an Italian Marinade, roast goose, red cabbage Scandinavian fashion and some other delights done as only Jehane can do them. She is Canada's cooking guru who lives up to her reputation and has also made the whole country eat better through her TV shows and writing. We came home early and slept well.

And then there is the annual party that becomes a tradition. Before retiring to Sidney, B.C. to grow tons of vegetables (with which to feed all the Easterners who zero in on them for visits) Doyle and Bill Klyn used to turn their large brownstone house in Westmount over to about 100 friends. Doyle is one of Canada's best-known magazine writers. Many of the guests were in the media, the people were interesting so the party was fun.

Doyle, who grew up in the West during the Depression, is a great cook and her simple but traditional menu was baked beans, roast ham, pickles, garlic bread, salads and her excellent butter tarts (their recipe is in this book). When the Klyns moved away, we stopped going out on New Year's Eve. We now stay home, watch brilliant and funny Dominique Michel give her annual New Year's Eve party on French TV and toast the New Year with a small glass of cognac.

However, if I were to have a party I think I'd serve the following:

> **French Onion Soup**
> **Pâté Maison**
> **Baker's French Bread**
> **Green Salad**
> **Trifle with Boiled Custard**
> **Coffee (lots of pots of it)**

OPENING THE COTTAGE

Lucky for us that Queen Victoria celebrated her birthday on
May 24th and that Quebec honors Dollard des Ormeaux on
this date too for it gives those with cottages a chance to spend
ā long weekend early in the season taking off storm windows,
cleaning up the grounds, putting wharves back in the water
and — if the house hasn't been used all winter — sweeping out
dead mice and airing damp rooms. Since you're going to be
busy, the first consideration is to bring along food that can be
reheated and stretched over two or three meals.

> Vichyssoise (Potato and Leek Soup)
> Beef Ragôut
> Herb Bread
> Doyle's Tarts

PICNICS

Eating out-of-doors in Canada is as old as the first settler who
had to eat that way till he'd built his log cabin, but picnics
came to their peak in our history during Sir John A. Macdonald's
time when he staged his political talks at huge outdoor feasts,
catered by small-town ladies and featuring, to paraphrase one
historian, "rancid food, noisy children and the nauseating
floods of oratory."

Today, politicians are inclined to stay indoors and though it
is hard to find the quiet, shady nook by the running stream,
picnics are still my favourite summer outing. The basic rule of
the menu is not to carry anything that melts or turns sour.
Even when you bring a picnic hamper that holds ice packs, it
is wise to select recipes that travel well.

> Stuffed Eggs
> Veal and Ham Pâté
> Sweet Gherkins
> Mrs. Macleod's Oatcakes
> Apples, bananas, oranges
> A bottle of wine

GREY CUP DAY

On a Sunday in late November all of Canada turns its back on the outdoors to gather in front of television screens for the Grey Cup. When the Canadian Football League championship game is over, it is re-played by the sedentary experts who find they've worked up quite an appetite. Since everyone in the household seems to become a football fan at least for that day, the menu is usually restricted to what can be prepared ahead of time — soup and home-made bread, to which home-made pecan pie is sometimes added. This is also the sort of snack which we find satisfying after skiing, snow-shoeing, curling, skating and shovelling the driveway, five activities which help Canadians survive the winter.

THANKSGIVING

Being farther to the North and, therefore, into cold weather sooner than the United States, Canadians celebrate Thanksgiving the second Monday in October. By that time, our harvest is in and the gardens and fields have been turned over for a seven-month rest.

Canadian Thanksgiving is pretty traditional.

> Roast Turkey
> Puréed Turnips
> Casserole of Onions
> Monique's Duchesse Potatoes
> Herbed Garden Carrots
> Cranberry Orange Relish
> Maple Syrup Pie

French-Canadian Cuisine

I was brought up in Ottawa in a French-Irish home — which is
the best way I know of acquiring a split personality. It is
really the best of all worlds — joie de vivre and fiery tempers.
At Christmas we always leaned toward the traditions of French
Canada, but when it came to wakes and weddings our Irish side
prevailed. Either way it was lively.

Our house was known for a marvellous Réveillon after Midnight
Mass on Christmas Eve. Most of the guests were my parents'
non-French, non-churchy friends who would turn up every
year to join the family at Mass and afterwards come to the
house for Réveillon. How wonderful it was to be finally old
enough to leave my childhood watching post at the top of the
stairs to come down and be part of the fun. When I visit
Ottawa I still meet people who remember those times and ask,
"Helen, do Irene and Ed still have Réveillons? " Yes, though
they've been modified considerably. My husband and I have
retained the traditions concerning food at holiday times for I
believe the best memories of childhood are made of such
pleasures.

FRENCH-CANADIAN PEA SOUP

In New England, this soup has been adapted to use a ham bone, but I really prefer the flavour of an authentic pea soup from Old Quebec — made with salt pork.

1 lb. dry peas	1 large onion minced
1 tbsp. coarse salt	1 tbsp. butter
1 to 2 lb. salt pork (fat and lean)	1 tsp. summer savory

Wash and sort peas.

Soak peas overnight in enough cold water to cover. The next morning measure the water in which peas have soaked and add enough to make 4 quarts.

Add salt to peas and water.

Saute onion in butter and add to peas.

Add savory.

Add pork in one piece.

Bring to a boil, cover, and simmer over low heat for 2 to 3 hours, or till peas are tender. Remove pork when it is tender (after 1 1/2 hours), cool on a plate, wrap in foil and store in freezer or refrigerator.

When peas are tender remove about 2 cups of the peas, blend or press through sieve and return to soup pot. This removes the watery look from the soup and gives it a richer texture. Leave remainder of peas whole.

The piece of pork makes an excellent main course and is best served very cold. It should be sliced very thin and eaten with hot bread and pickles, the French-Canadian way.

OLD QUEBEC SALMON PUDDING

1 tbsp. butter
1 1/2 tbsp. flour
1/2 cup milk
1-lb. tin salmon
1 stalk celery, chopped
1 small onion, chopped
Few sprigs parsley

1/8 tsp. pepper
1 tbsp. dry mustard
1 tsp. salt
3 tbsp. evaporated milk
2 eggs, separated
1 pkg. green peas, fresh or canned

Heat oven to 350 degrees and grease a medium-size casserole.

Melt butter in a saucepan, stir in flour until smooth, then add milk gradually and cook over low heat, stirring constantly until sauce is smooth and slightly thick.

Drain salmon and separate it into small pieces with a fork.

Add salmon to white sauce with celery, onion and parsley.

Add pepper, mustard, salt, evaporated milk and slightly beaten egg yolks.

Beat egg whites until they hold a peak, then mix very gently into salmon mixture.

Transfer to casserole and bake for 35 minutes.

Serve with hot peas. (Serves 4.)

OLD QUEBEC DINNER-IN-A-POT

4 thick pork chops
4 medium-sized potatoes, pared
    and sliced in 1/2-inch slices
Salt and pepper (to taste)

4 medium-sized onions, pared and
    sliced
2 cups milk

Remove excess fat from pork chops. Dice and melt this fat until brown.

Fry chops in melted fat over quick heat for about 5 minutes on each side.

Place chops in bottom of baking dish.

Cover with potatoes and onions and sprinkle with salt and pepper.

Pour milk over top. Cover and bake for 2 hours in a 350-degree oven.

15

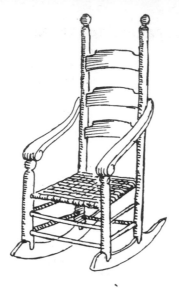

TOURTIÈRE

This is the famous Quebec minced pork pie associated with the early Christmas morning réveillon. Some cooks combine minced beef with pork and it makes a good pie, but can't be called a real tourtière.

1 lb. minced fresh pork	1/2 tsp. savory
1 small onion, diced	1/4 tsp. celery pepper
1 small garlic clove	1/4 tsp. cloves
1/2 tsp. salt	1/2 cup water

Combine ingredients in a Dutch oven or other heavy pot and bring to the boil.

Reduce heat and cook uncovered for 20 minutes, or long enough to remove the pink tone from the meat and to reduce most of the water. The mixture should be damp but not watery. Remove garlic clove.

Cool mixture and pour into unbaked pie shell (recipe follows). Cover with pastry and prick to allow steam to escape.

Bake at 450 degrees for 10 minutes, then reduce oven heat to 350 degrees and bake till crust is light brown. The pie is eaten hot and is delicious with chili sauce or other relishes.

If desired, the unbaked tourtière may be frozen and baked weeks later. (Makes 1 9-inch pie.)

PASTRY FOR TOURTIÈRE

2 1/4 cups all-purpose flour, sifted   3/4 cup lard OR vegetable shortening
1 tsp. salt   5 1/2 tbsp. cold water

Sift a quantity of all-purpose flour on a piece of waxpaper. Set empty flour sifter in medium mixing bowl.

Measure 2 cups sifted flour back into sifter. Add salt and sift into bowl.

Drop lard or shortening into flour.

Cut shortening into flour, using two knives, one in each hand. Work knives in criss-cross fashion, like scissors, until flour-coated particles are size of peas. Or use pastry blender.

Slowly stir cold water into remaining 1/4 cup sifted flour in small bowl. Mix until smooth. Add to shortening mixture, stirring with two-tined fork, until particles stick together when gently pressed with fork.

Form pastry gently into a ball in a bowl, place on a piece of wax-paper. Wrap up and chill half an hour — no longer — before using.

Roll out pastry. (Makes 2 9-inch pie crusts.)

ROAST FRESH SHOULDER OF PORK
WITH APPLE STUFFING

Have your butcher remove the bone from a shoulder of pork.

Spread stuffing (recipe follows) on meat. Roll like a jelly roll. Secure with string.

Place roast on a rack in pan. Add removed bone to pan and place in a 350-degree oven.

Bake uncovered, 45 minutes to the pound. Turn every half hour.

APPLE STUFFING

1/4 cup salt pork, diced
1/2 cup celery, chopped
1/2 cup onion, chopped
1/4 cup parsley, chopped

5 apples, diced
1/3 cup sugar
2 cups dry bread crumbs

Fry salt pork until crisp. Remove from skillet.

Cook celery, onion and parsley in fat for 5 minutes. Remove from skillet.

Place apples in skillet and sprinkle with sugar. Cook, covered, until tender.

Remove cover and continue to cook until juice evaporates. Add bread crumbs and other ingredients and mix well.

QUEBEC POTATO PIE

This is one of my favourite Lenten meals. I have used canned deep-sea trout instead of salmon and enjoyed it, too. Prepare it in the morning and store in the refrigerator till dinner-time if you have a busy day planned.

Pie crust
6 medium-sized potatoes,
   peeled and boiled
3 tbsp. butter
1/2 tsp. savory
2 tbsp. parsley, minced

1/4 tsp. mint, chopped (optional)
Salt and pepper (to taste)
2 medium-sized onions, sliced
1 tbsp. fat
1 8-oz. tin salmon

Line a baking dish with pie crust.

Mash potatoes with butter, savory, parsley and mint. Season with salt and pepper. (Do not add any liquid to the potatoes.)

Place mashed potatoes in baking dish.

Fry onions in fat until brown. Spread over potatoes.

Top onions with undrained flaked canned salmon and cover with a second pie crust, which has a few small slits.

Brush top crust with a little milk.

Bake in a 400-degree oven for 20 to 25 minutes or until golden brown in colour. (Serves 6.)

HEAD CHEESE

1/2 or 1 head of pork	2 large onions, chopped
6 cloves	1 large carrot, grated
1 tbsp. cinnamon	2 qts. hot water
2 tbsp. salt	

Wrap head of pork in a cloth. Place in a pot with cloves, cinnamon, salt, onions, carrot and hot water.

Bring to a boil. Cover and cook over low heat for 2 hours. Unwrap the head and chop the boned meat.

Place in hot broth and cook over high heat for 10 minutes.

Pour into moulds and cool until head cheese is set.

(Serves 8 to 10)

PÂTÉ CHINOIS

It's called Shepherd's Pie in all the other provinces, but in Québec its nationality has been changed and the French-Canadian custom of adding a layer of creamed corn under the potatoes makes it a very popular one-dish meal.

4 tbsp. butter	1 can creamed corn
1 1/2 lb. minced beef, fresh	3 cups mashed potatoes
1 onion, chopped	Butter
Salt and pepper	

Melt butter and cook onion in it till golden. Add meat and stir till all trace of pink is gone. Salt to taste.

Pour meat and onion into greased casserole, spread corn over top and spoon or pipe mashed potatoes, salted and peppered to taste, over top. Sprinkle with paprika and dot with butter. Bake in 375 degree oven for 25 to 30 minutes. Serves 6.

ROAST PORK WITH GRAISSE DE RÔTI

One of the great pioneer delicacies of Québec was the fat from roast pork with its natural jelly. This was eaten by hungry men and children spread onto bread and sprinkled with salt and pepper. I hadn't had any for years until the night Madame Lucette Lapointe appeared on "Bon Appétit" and showed how it is still done. Pork cooks best in a black cast-iron casserole but if you want your "graisse" to be pure white, use a heavy enamelled-iron casserole.

4-5 lb. loin of pork with filet
2 garlic cloves
1 1/2 tsp. salt

1/2 tsp. pepper
1 envelope plain gelatine

Have the butcher saw the pork loin bones to make it easier for slicing and ask him for extra fat and rind to make the dish a greater success.

Wipe roast with a damp cloth and cut slits into the fat and insert garlic slices. Sprinkle with salt and pepper.

Place extra fat and rind in the casserole and heat. When it starts to melt, place the roast in the fat and brown it on all sides to a deep gold, sprinkle with salt and pepper and add 5 cups of water for a 5-lb. roast — or one cup per lb. of meat. Brown roast, then cover pot tightly and cook roast on top of stove for 3 to 4 hours, turning it once in a while.

Remove cover during the last half hour. Taste and add more salt and pepper if necessary. When you can stick a long fork or skewer into the roast, it is ready.

Remove roast and boil up remaining liquid. Dilute the gelatine in 1/3 cup of consommé over low heat. Remove from heat, add to pork liquid. Stir off heat, and pass through a sieve into a pretty mold. Cool before putting in the fridge. Eat with crusty bread.

BRAWN

3 lb. pigs' knuckles
Half a pig's head
3 quarts hot water
1 large onion
2 carrots
2 cloves
1 tbsp. salt

8 to 10 stems parsley
Handful of celery leaves
2 bay leaves
1/2 cup vinegar
1/2 lb. smoked tongue
1/2 cup chopped pickles

Place pigs' knuckles with half a pig's head in a large saucepan. Cover with hot water.

Add large onion, carrots, cloves, salt, parsley, celery leaves, bay leaves and vinegar. Bring to a boil and simmer very slowly for 3 hours or until meat is quite soft.

Strain liquid into a bowl and leave to cool.

Remove all meat from bones and chop very finely.

Add smoked tongue, cut in long slivers.

Remove all fat from cold liquid, add to meat and boil together. Bring the whole to a boil, then remove from fire.

Let cool gradually, stirring often to keep meat well mixed in the jelly.

When cold, add chopped pickles. Also taste the liquid when cold and add more seasoning, if necessary, and a little more vinegar, as the brawn should be quite sharp.

Pour into wet moulds and set in cold place.

Unmould and serve cut into slices.

Sprinkle with finely chopped onion and a dressing of oil and vinegar.

PIGS' KNUCKLES IN BROWN SAUCE

2 to 3 lb. pigs' knuckles
1 tsp. coarse salt
1/4 tsp. pepper
1/2 tsp. cinnamon
1/4 tsp. ground cloves
Pinch of nutmeg

2 tbsp. fat
6 cups tepid water
1 cup onions, lightly fried
1/2 cup browned flour
1 cup cold water

Cut pigs' knuckles into individual pieces.

Roll each piece in a mixture of coarse salt, pepper, cinnamon, ground cloves and nutmeg.

Melt fat and brown knuckles in it until they are a good brown colour. Add tepid water and fried onions.

Cover and simmer until meat is tender (about 2 to 2 1/2 hours).

Thicken with brown flour diluted in cold water.

RAGOÛT DE BOULETTES

1 lb. fresh lean pork, ground
1/2 lb. beef, ground
1/4 lb. salt pork (or less)
1 small onion, minced
2 tbsp. parsley
1/4 tsp. powdered ginger
1/4 tsp. cinnamon
1/4 tsp. cloves

1/4 tsp. dry mustard
2 slices of bread
1/2 cup milk
Salt and pepper
3 tbsp. bacon fat OR shortening
3 cups water
4 tbsp. browned flour
1/2 cup water

Pass meat 3 times through meat grinder or have the butcher do it.

Add onion, parsley, spices and mustard.

Soak cubed bread in milk and add to meat.

Add salt and pepper and roll mixture in palms of hands into little balls.

Fry meat balls in fat and when all are browned add 3 cups of water. Cover and boil gently for half an hour.

Shake browned flour and 1/2 cup water together in a fruit sealer or put into blender.

Add to meat-ball mixture and cook, while stirring, until gravy is thickened slightly.

Serve in a large casserole with boiled potatoes. (Serves 6.)

QUEBEC SALT PORK AND CABBAGE

2 lb. lean and fat salt pork
2 large onions, sliced
1 tsp. salt
1/4 tsp. pepper
1/2 tsp. savory

2 whole cloves
2 quarts cold water
1 medium-sized cabbage, quartered
6 to 8 potatoes

Place pork, onions, salt, pepper, savory, whole cloves and cold water in a large saucepan. Bring to a boil, then simmer, covered, until pork is tender (about 1 1/2 to 2 hours).

Add cabbage and potatoes during the last half-hour of cooking.

To serve, place the drained cabbage in a platter, surround with the drained potatoes and garnish with the sliced pork. (Serves 6.)

ROAST QUEBEC DUCK

Many women have asked me for ways of cooking duck because most cook books, out of the gourmet class, seem to ignore this bird. Two recipes for Duck a l'Orange, found in the chapter on fowl and game, and this one are among the best I've ever tried.

3 medium apples
1/2 tsp. salt
1/4 tsp. pepper
1/4 tsp. cloves
1/4 tsp. cinnamon
1/4 tsp. nutmeg

1/4 tsp. dry mustard
1 duck
2 thin slices salt pork
1 cup apple juice
1 onion, minced

Peel and quarter apples and roll each piece in a mixture of salt, pepper, cloves, cinnamon, nutmeg and mustard.

Place apples in the cavity of the duck and sew it up.

Spread slices of salt pork over the duck's breast. Sprinkle bird with salt and pepper.

Place in a heavy casserole with apple juice and onion.

Roast in a 450-degree oven about an hour, uncovered.

Thicken gravy if desired, as you would chicken gravy.

BEEF RAGOÛT

2 lb. beef (short rib or brisket)	1 tsp. salt
2 tbsp. butter	1/4 tsp. pepper
1 onion, minced	2 cups Canadian red wine
2 carrots, diced	2 1/2 cups water OR consommé
1 stick celery, diced	1 tbsp. parsley
2 tbsp. flour (browned)	1/4 tsp. thyme OR savory
3 fresh tomatoes	1 bay leaf
2 cloves garlic, chopped finely	

Cut meat into 2-inch cubes.

Fry in butter until golden brown.

Add onion, carrots and celery and continue cooking until vegetables start to brown slightly.

Add flour and mix well.

Add tomatoes (cut in small pieces) and remaining ingredients.

Cover and cook over low heat until beef is tender (about 3 hours), or cook for the same length of time in a 300-degree oven.

Serve with boiled potatoes or noodles.   (Serves 4 to 6.)

FILLET OF SOLE CHÂTEAU FRONTENAC

4 fillets of sole	3 tbsp. water, apple juice
1 green onion, chopped	OR clam juice
1 tbsp. parsley, chopped	1 tbsp. butter
6 mushrooms, sliced	3 tbsp. cream, hot
Salt and pepper (to taste)	1 tsp. lemon juice
	1 tbsp. butter cut in small pieces

Take 4 nice fillets of sole and place them in a buttered fish dish that has been sprinkled with a chopped shallot and a little chopped parsley.

Add a few sliced mushrooms and salt and pepper.

Add water, apple juice or clam juice, top with a few pieces of butter and cover with a piece of brown paper cut the same size as the dish.

Bake in a 500-degree oven for 15 minutes.

When cooked remove the fish gravy to another pan and reduce it to one third over quick heat.

Add to the reduced stock the hot cream, lemon juice and butter.

Mix well, taste for seasoning and pour over filets.

Place in a 550-degree oven or under direct flame until brown here and there (about 5 minutes).

The fish should be served in the dish in which it is baked. (Serves 4.)

QUEBEC BAKED BEANS

4 cups dry beans (2 lb.)	1 large onion
1 tsp. baking soda	Dry mustard
1/2 to 1 lb. salt pork, diced	1/2 cup molasses

Soak beans in cold water (to cover) for at least 3 hours. Rinse.

Cover with fresh, cold water, add soda and bring to a boil. Boil for half an hour. Rinse well.

Put two slices of pork in the bottom of an earthenware pot (preferably a bean pot).

Pour beans into the pot. Bury the onion, rolled in dry mustard, in the middle of the beans.

Pour molasses over all. Cover with remaining pork slices and add enough hot water to cover the beans. Cover pot.

Bake for 4 hours (or more if desired) at 375 degrees.

One hour before beans are finished, add a little water if they look dry. Cover may be removed during the last half-hour if a crisp surface is desired.

SUGAR PIE

This recipe for Sugar Pie done on my TV show by Marcel Beaulieu, the chef at Molson's Brewery, is one of the traditional sweets of Québec.

1 cup water	1 3/4 cups whipping cream
1 cup white sugar	1/2 cup flour
1 cup brown sugar	1/2 cup butter

Combine in a heavy pot water and sugars and bring to the boil, simmering 7 to 8 minutes.

Heat cream in a second pot, add to sugar mixture and simmer an additional 8 minutes.

Melt butter in a heavy frypan, add flour to make a roux and stir over low heat with a whisk for a few minutes but do not brown.

Add cream mixture, a little at a time, stirring all the time, till all cream has been added and mixture is smooth.

Cool, pour into an unbaked pie shell, cover with a pie top (or leave it off if you prefer). Bake at 350 to 375 degrees for 25 to 30 minutes.

Serve at room temperature with ice cream.

APPLE CIDER PIE

6 medium tart apples	1/2 tsp. cinnamon
1 to 2 cups cider	1/4 tsp. ground nutmeg
Flour	1/4 tsp. ground cloves
1/2 cup sugar	1 pie shell

Peel and core apples and cut into eighths.

Place apples in pot and cover with cider.

Cook over slow fire for approximately 30 minutes, or till soft.

Remove from heat and if the sauce is not thick add a little flour.

Add sugar and spices.

Bake a pie shell for about 5 minutes, then pour apple filling into it. Cover top, lattice-fashion, with uncooked pastry strips and bake at 450 degrees for 8 minutes. Reduce heat to 350 degrees and bake 25 minutes longer.

OLD-FASHIONED BLUEBERRY PUDDING

3 cups fresh blueberries OR 2 pkgs.
    frozen blueberries
1/3 cup cold water
1 tsp. gelatin
1/4 cup boiling water

1/2 cup sugar
1 tsp. lemon juice
7 thin slices bread
1/2 cup butter, melted

Place fresh berries in a saucepan with cold water and cook 5 minutes till berries are tender. Or thaw frozen blueberries and do not add any water.

Soften gelatin in 1/4 cup of juice from cooked or frozen blueberries and let stand for 5 minutes.

Dissolve gelatin mixture in boiling water, add sugar, lemon juice, berries and berry juice.

Cut crusts from bread and brush both sides of bread generously with melted butter (a pastry brush is handy for this).

Line bottom and sides of a 1-quart dish with bread (cutting slices to make a neat effect). Remaining slices should be cut into small, neat squares for topping.

Spoon a third of the berry mixture over lining of bread, arrange a layer of bread squares on top, repeat with berry mixture and bread topping till all is used.

Place in refrigerator and chill all day.

Serve with whipped cream or sour cream. (Serves 6 to 8.)

CANADIAN MAPLE SYRUP PIE

1 tbsp. gelatin
2 tbsp. cold water
1/2 cup milk
1/2 cup maple syrup
1/4 tsp. salt

2 eggs separated
1 1/2 cups whipping cream
1 tsp. vanilla
1 baked pie shell

Soften gelatin in cold water.

Heat milk, maple syrup and salt in top of a double boiler. When warm, slowly add well-beaten egg yolks.

Add gelatin and stir until dissolved.   Cool mixture.

Whip cream and flavour with vanilla.

Place half of whipped cream to one side.   Whip egg whites and add to cool custard.   Add one half of whipping cream.

Pour mixture into baked pie shell and top with whipped cream that was set aside.

Store in refrigerator until very cold.

Canada's Multicultural Kitchens

Canadian cooking has always borrowed, adopted and adapted foods
from other countries; we are hardly aware of the exotic origins of
some of our most popular recipes.

Some foods from other lands, however, have retained their
identity, and these I have grouped in this chapter. After all
when you're eating curry, you want to feel you're tasting
Calcutta, not Calgary.

The Chinese and the Italians have had a strong influence on
Canadian cookery, and the result is that our supermarkets are
stocked with the special ingredients which Oriental and Latin
dishes require. Hungarian specialties are popular, particularly
in the cities which have absorbed large numbers of immigrants.
Hungarian friends in Montreal, Toronto and Vancouver tell
me that some of the goulashes served here are better than
they last tasted in Budapest. A sample of their old-world
politeness, perhaps, but one thing I do know — a well-made
goulash is delicious.

LASAGNE

1 large onion	1 lb. ground beef
1 clove garlic	1 small onion
6 sprigs parsley	4 tbsp. butter, margarine
1/4 cup olive oil OR salad oil	OR shortening
1 large can tomatoes	3 tbsp. flour
1 can (4 oz.) tomato paste	3/4 cup grated Parmesan cheese
2 bay leaves	2 cups milk
1 tsp. salt	2 egg yolks
1/4 tsp. pepper	1/2 lb. lasagne noodles
1/2 cup water	

TOMATO SAUCE

Chop onion, garlic and parsley finely and fry slightly in hot oil. Add tomatoes, tomato paste, bay leaves, salt, pepper and water and stir until well mixed. Then toss in the ground beef, breaking it up into little pieces with a fork or spoon.

Cover and cook over low heat for 45 minutes, giving it an occasional stir.

CHEESE SAUCE

Chop small onion finely and cook in melted butter, margarine or shortening 1 to 2 minutes.

Mix in the flour smoothly, add cheese and a dash of salt.

Gradually stir in the milk and continue cooking over low heat, stirring constantly, until sauce is as thick as heavy cream.

Beat egg yolks slightly, mix in a little hot cheese mixture slowly to prevent sauce from curdling, then mix all the cheese mixture and yolks together and cook over low heat for 10 minutes longer. Remove from fire.

Cook noodles as directed on package, then drain.

Start oven at 325 degrees and grease a large baking dish.

Put a layer of noodles on the bottom of the baking dish, pour over enough tomato sauce to cover noodles and add some of the cheese sauce to this. Continue layers until ingredients are all used. Finish with a covering of cheese sauce. Bake 20 minutes, then set oven to broil and broil till surface is golden. (Serves 6 to 8.)

MEATBALL SPAGHETTI SAUCE

2 medium-sized onions	3/4 lb. beef, minced
3 tbsp. salad oil or bacon fat	1/4 lb. pork, minced
1 No. 2 tin tomatoes (2 1/2 cups)	1 cup fine, dry, white bread crumbs
2 6-oz. tins tomato paste	1/2 cup grated cheese
2 cups water	1 sprig parsley, minced
1 tsp. salt	1 clove garlic, minced
1/2 tsp. pepper	1/2 cup milk
1 tbsp. sugar	2 eggs, well beaten
1 bay leaf	1/2 tsp. salt
1/2 tsp. marjoram	1/4 tsp. pepper
1/2 tsp. savory	Paprika

Brown onions in salad oil or bacon fat. Add tomatoes, tomato paste, water, 1 tsp. salt, 1/2 tsp. pepper, sugar, bay leaf, marjoram and savory and bring to a boil. Cover and simmer for 1 hour.

Blend in a bowl beef, pork, bread crumbs, cheese, parsley, garlic, milk, eggs, 1/2 tsp. salt and 1/4 tsp. pepper. When thoroughly mixed form into small balls.

Sprinkle generously with paprika and brown quickly in salad oil or bacon fat just long enough to remove rawness.

Add to sauce 10 minutes before serving. (Sufficient for 16 oz. spaghetti.)

SPAGHETTI SAUCE FOR FREEZING

1 cup olive oil
4 large onions, thinly sliced
6 cloves garlic, chopped
2 green peppers, cut into squares
1 small head celery (including leaves), sliced
1 lb. minced beef OR chicken liver OR calf's liver
2 large tins (20 oz.) tomatoes

1 6-oz. tin tomato paste
1/2 cup minced parsley
1 tsp. rosemary
1 tsp. marjoram
2 tsp. basil
1/2 to 1 lb. thinly sliced fresh mushrooms
2 tbsp. sugar

Heat olive oil and add onions, garlic, peppers, celery and meat. Stir and cook over medium heat for 20 minutes.

Add remaining ingredients.

Simmer over low heat, covered, for 2 to 3 hours until the consistency that you prefer has been reached.

Cool before packaging. Store in portions in freezer, and keep from 2 to 8 months. Thaw in double boiler. (Makes 20 portions.)

POT-AU-FEU

2 1/2 lb. beef brisket, neck
    or chuck
1 small soup bone, cracked
2 qts. cold water
2 1/2 cups carrots, diced
4 onions, sliced
4 stalks celery, diced

2 1/2 cups potatoes, diced
2 cups turnips, diced
2 tbsp. parsley, chopped
2 tsp. salt
Pepper
Crisp toast OR French bread

Cut beef into pieces and add with soup bone to water. Bring slowly to a boil, cover tightly and simmer gently for 4 or 5 hours.

Add vegetables, parsley and salt, bring to a boil and simmer, covered, for 1 1/2 hours longer.

Remove beef and bone, cut meat into small pieces and return to soup.

Let stand until cold and fat hardens on top.

Remove fat and reheat soup. Season with salt and pepper if necessary.

Serve hot with crisp toast or spread rounds of toasted French bread with butter and place one in each soup bowl before filling with hot soup. Other meat such as veal, lamb or chicken may be substituted for beef. This is a hearty dish which can be eaten as a main course. (Serves 4 to 6.)

COQUILLES SAINT JACQUES

8 large scallops (fresh or frozen)
4 tbsp. butter OR margarine
1 tbsp. green onions, chopped
1/4 lb. sliced fresh mushrooms
   (or a 3-to-4 oz. can)
3 tbsp. flour
1 cup white wine OR chicken
   OR fish stock

1 tsp. parsley, chopped
1/4 tsp. thyme
1/4 tsp. basil
Salt and pepper
1/2 cup cream
1/4 cup fine, dry bread crumbs

Drain scallops on paper towelling and cut into 1/2-inch cubes.

Heat 2 tbsp. of butter or margarine in heavy skillet over medium heat. Add scallops, onion and mushrooms and cook until vegetables are soft.

Combine flour and wine with parsley, thyme, basil, salt and pepper and add to scallops, blending well.

Reduce heat and cook slowly, about 10 minutes, stirring occasionally.

Stir in cream and cook 1 minute longer.

Pour mixture into 4 buttered, individual shells or baking dishes.

Melt remaining 2 tbsp. butter or margarine and combine with bread crumbs; sprinkle on top of mixture.

Bake in moderate oven (350 degrees) for about 20 minutes or until bubbly.

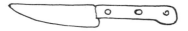

POULE AU CHOU (Chicken and Cabbage Stew)

1/2 lb. salt pork
1 fowl
Flour
1 large green cabbage
4 to 6 large onions

1 tsp. salt
1/4 tsp. pepper
1/2 tsp. thyme
1/2 cup water

Dice and melt salt pork. Cut fowl into serving pieces and roll each piece in flour until well covered.

Brown in melted fat, and when browned remove pieces of chicken.

Chop green cabbage coarsely and slice onions thinly.

Place cabbage and onions in remaining fat and cook over medium heat, stirring often, until the vegetables have softened (approximately 15 minutes).

Place pieces of chicken over cabbage. Add salt, pepper, thyme and water.

Cover tightly and cook over low heat for at least 2 hours. (Serves 4 to 6.)

CHICKEN SAUTÉ CHASSEUR

1 2 1/2-to-3-lb. broiler or young chicken, cut into individual pieces	1/4 lb. mushrooms, chopped
	2 tbsp. lemon juice
	1 tsp. sugar
Flour seasoned with salt and pepper	1 tsp. salt
	1/3 cup apple juice
1/4 tsp. thyme	2 medium-sized tomatoes, diced
Butter	Parsley or chives
4 green onions, minced	

Roll chicken in seasoned flour to which thyme has also been added.

Brown chicken in butter, turning occasionally so that it will be brown on both sides.

Add shallots, mushrooms, lemon juice, sugar, salt, apple juice and tomatoes when chicken is browned.

Cover frying pan and cook over low heat for 40 to 60 minutes or until chicken is tender. Uncover and sprinkle with parsley or chives. (Serves 3 to 5.)

FRENCH MEAT LOAF

1 lb. ground beef	2 eggs, beaten
1 lb. ground pork	1/2 cup fresh bread crumbs
1 lb. ground veal	Milk
1/2 cup green onions, chopped	1/2 tsp. rosemary OR sage
1/2 cup parsley, chopped	Pinch of nutmeg
1 tsp. salt	Bacon strips
1 1/2 tsp. pepper	

Combine ground meat with onions, parsley, salt, pepper beaten eggs and bread crumbs (which have been soaked in a little milk), rosemary or sage and a pinch of nutmeg.

Mix thoroughly with the hands.

Shape into a loaf and place on a layer of bacon strips in an earthenware baking dish, casserole or loaf pan.

Top with a few strips of bacon and bake uncovered at 325 degrees for 1 1/2 to 2 hours. This is delicious hot, but much better pressed and served cold. Press with a weight (a heavy flat stone or iron placed on a plate covering loaf). (Serves 10 to 12.)

LIVER LOAF DAUPHINOISE

1/2 lb. calf, beef OR chicken liver	1 cup white sauce (recipe follows)
2 cloves garlic, chopped	1/2 tsp. salt
Several sprigs parsley, chopped	Pepper (to taste)
1 small onion, chopped	Tomato sauce (recipe follows)
4 eggs	

Chop liver very finely through a chopper, if possible. Add garlic, parsley and onion to liver.

Separate eggs. Mix yolks with white sauce and add chopped meat mixture. Season with salt and pepper.

Beat egg whites very stiff and fold in slowly.

Butter a casserole, fill with mixture and bake in a 300-degree oven for about an hour. A knife inserted into the loaf will come out dry if the loaf is cooked.

Turn loaf out on a glass oven baking dish, cover with tomato sauce and return to oven for a few minutes. (Serves 6.)

TOMATO SAUCE

1 20-oz. tin tomatoes

Butter

Black olives (optional)

Sautéed mushrooms (optional)

Heat butter in a saucepan. Empty tomatoes into saucepan and cook lightly.

Add olives and mushrooms if desired.

WHITE OR BECHAMEL SAUCE

3 tbsp. butter OR margarine

2 tbsp. flour

1 cup milk

1/2 tbsp. butter

Melt butter or margarine. Add flour and mix well.

Add milk gradually, season and stir continually for about 10 minutes until well thickened. Remove from heat and add butter.

FRENCH CHICKEN CASSEROLE

1 roasting chicken

1 strip bacon OR salt pork

Salt and pepper

4 potatoes

4 onions

4 carrots

3 tomatoes, halved

12 mushrooms

Vegetables (any kind but beets)

2 bay leaves

Pinch of rosemary

1/2 cup of water

Spread bacon or pork on bottom of deep casserole and place chicken, cut into serving pieces, on it. Sprinkle with salt and pepper.

Arrange vegetables (cut up potatoes, onions and carrots, if you wish) and add any vegetables you have in the house — turnips, cauliflower, celery, green pepper, green beans, lima beans are ideal.

Season vegetables as you place them in the dish, thick vegetables on the bottom and green vegetables, mushrooms and tomatoes on top, cut side up.

Add bay leaves, rosemary and water.

Cover and place in a 375-degree oven and leave for 1 1/2 to 2 hours. If there is too much liquid, uncover casserole during last half hour. (Serves 4.)

SPANISH CHICKEN STEW

2 fryers, cut up
1 1/2 tsp. salt
1/2 tsp. freshly ground black
   pepper
1 1/2 tsp. paprika
1/4 cup olive oil
1 cup onions, diced
1 bay leaf
1/2 cup dry Spanish sherry

1 clove garlic, minced
2 potatoes, pared and cubed
1 can (No. 1) tiny peas, drained
   OR 1 package frozen peas
1/4 cup green olives, sliced
1/4 cup pimientos, sliced
1/4 cup almonds, blanched and
   sliced

Combine salt, pepper and paprika. Season the chicken with the mixture the day before it is used, if possible.

Heat the oil in a skillet. Brown the chicken pieces in it and then transfer them to a casserole or heavy saucepan.

Sauté the onions in the fat remaining in the skillet for 10 minutes, stirring frequently. Add to the chicken with the bay leaf and sherry. Cover and cook over low heat for 1 hour.

Add the garlic and potatoes. Cover and cook over low heat for 15 minutes. Add a little more sherry, if necessary.

Add the peas, olives, pimientos and almonds; cook for another 15 minutes. Correct seasoning. (Serves 6.)

Note: Delicious with a crisp green salad and glasses of chilled sherry, sherry and soda, or sherry on the rocks.

PAELLA VALENCIANA

1 2-to-3-lb. broiler, cut into individual pieces
1/4 cup salad oil
2 large onions, chopped finely
2 cloves garlic, minced
2 green peppers, cut into 1-inch pieces
2 cups uncooked rice
1 tin (28 oz.) tomatoes
2 cups hot water
1 tsp. turmeric OR 1/2 tsp. saffron

1/4 cup hot water
1 to 1 1/2 lb. lobster OR 2 8-oz. tins of lobster
1 lb. fresh shrimps OR 2 6-oz. tins of shrimp
1 tin clams
1 dry garlic sausage, sliced OR 1/2 lb. pre-cooked fresh sausages
1/4 to 1/2 cup sherry (optional)
1 box frozen green peas
Salt and pepper (to taste)

Brown chicken slowly in salad oil in a very large saucepan or heavy Dutch Oven.

Add onions, garlic and green peppers.

Cover and simmer 20 minutes on very low heat.

Pour uncooked rice over chicken and vegetables. Add tomatoes, 2 cups hot water, turmeric or saffron dissolved in 1/4 cup of hot water. Stir till well mixed.

Cover and cook over low heat for about 20 minutes or until rice is tender.

Add lobster, shrimp and clams. When using fresh lobster and shrimp, clean them and add them raw to the rice and chicken. When using canned seafood, add to chicken undrained.

Add sausages, arranging them attractively.

Add sherry and cook together over low heat for another 20 minutes. Twenty minutes will be sufficient to cook the raw seafood.

Add hot cooked peas and season to taste. (Serves 6.)

Note: This makes a wonderful buffet dish. It can be prepared a day ahead or frozen.

BEEF STROGANOFF

3 lb. tender beefsteak (tenderloin, sirloin or top round)
3 medium onions, chopped
4 tbsp. butter or margarine
1 lb. mushrooms, sliced

1/2 tsp. powdered or crushed basil
Salt and pepper (to taste)
1 cup sour cream (commercial)
1/2 tsp. grated nutmeg

Pound steak until it is thin, then cut into two-inch strips (3/4-inch thick).

Sauté onions in 2 tbsp. butter or margarine until they are only slightly brown.

Brown beef strips quickly, turning constantly to brown both sides (about 6 or 7 minutes), then remove them to a heated pan.

Add 2 tbsp. butter or margarine to the first pan and sauté the mushrooms until they are tender.

Return the beef to the pan and season with basil and salt and pepper. When this is piping hot, add sour cream and mix well, but do not allow it to boil.

To serve immediately, pour over fluffy rice and sprinkle with nutmeg. Paprika may be shaken over the top if you wish.

To freeze, pour into plastic boxes, cover securely and, when cool, place in freezer.

To prepare for serving, thaw in top of double boiler or in buttered casserole in the oven. Serve with rice as above. (Serves 6 to 8.)

HUNGARIAN BEEF STEW

5 onions, chopped
6 tbsp. butter OR margarine
2 lb. tender beef, cut in long strips
1/2 tsp. salt
Dash of marjoram
1/4 tsp. pepper

1 clove garlic, crushed
3/4 cup white wine OR consomme'
1/4 lb. bacon, sliced and diced
2 cups sour cream
Cooked noodles

Brown onions in butter or margarine.

Add meat and season with salt, marjoram, pepper and garlic. Stir in wine or consommé. Cover and simmer slowly for 25 minutes.

Brown bacon and add to meat.

Stir in sour cream, cover and continue cooking for about 20 minutes, or until meat is tender. Serve over cooked noodles. (Serves 6.)

HUNGARIAN GOULASH

4 tbsp. butter
5 to 6 onions, chopped
2 tbsp. Hungarian paprika
2 tsp. salt
1/2 tsp. pepper

3 lb. chuck beef, in 2" pieces
1 can tomato sauce
1 clove garlic, minced
1/2 cup sour cream

Sauté chopped onions in butter in a heavy pan about 15 minutes, stirring frequently. Remove onions and set aside.

Combine seasonings and roll meat, which has been cut into 2-inch cubes, in it.

If more butter is desired, add 2 tbsp. to pan and brown meat on all sides in it. Add sautéed onions, tomato sauce and garlic.

Stir, cover and cook over low heat for three hours, stirring now and then.

Add sour cream but do not boil again.

Serve with boiled noodles, sprinkled with poppy seed.

CABBAGE ROLLS

1 large cabbage
1 lb. chuck OR top round steak
   ground
1/4 cup cooked rice
2 tbsp. sugar
2 tbsp. grated onion
1 tbsp. fresh, frozen or canned
   lemon juice
1 1/2 tsp. salt

1/4 tsp. pepper
1/2 tsp. paprika
1 large onion, minced
2 tbsp. salad oil OR bacon fat
1/2 cup hot water
2 8-oz. tins tomato sauce
1/4 to 1/2 cup brown sugar
1/4 cup fresh, frozen or canned
   lemon juice

Wash cabbage, cut out the core end, separate leaves gently, pour boiling water over them and leave for 10 minutes.

Combine meat, rice, 2 tbsp. sugar, grated onion, 1 tbsp. lemon juice, 1 tsp. salt, 1/4 tsp. pepper and 1/4 tsp. paprika.

Drain cabbage leaves, place on wooden board, put a spoonful of meat mixture on each leaf and roll up, tuck in ends and use toothpicks if necessary.

Sauté minced onion with remaining 1/2 tsp. salt, 1/4 tsp. paprika and a dash of pepper in hot fat in frying pan or Dutch Oven for about 10 minutes.

Add hot water and transfer onion mixture to casserole or leave in Dutch Oven.

Arrange cabbage rolls on top of onion.

Mix tomato sauce with sugar and 1/4 cup lemon juice; pour over cabbage rolls.

Cover and bake for 2 to 3 hours in a 325-degree oven.

Taste and add more sugar and lemon juice if necessary. If cooked on top of stove do so over low heat. This recipe is better prepared a day in advance. (Serves 4 to 5.)

VIENNESE VEAL WITH SOUR CREAM AND NOODLES

1 1/2 to 2 lb. cubed veal
Salt and pepper
Monosodium glutamate (MSG)
1 small clove garlic
2 tbsp. butter OR olive oil

1 medium-sized onion, thinly sliced
1/2 cup water
Pinch of thyme
3/4 cup sour cream
8 oz. thin noodles

Cut veal into 1-inch cubes. Sprinkle with salt, pepper and monosodium glutamate.

Crush or chop garlic very finely.

Melt butter or olive oil in a heavy saucepan. When hot, sauté onions and garlic, then add veal cubes, onion, water and a pinch of thyme.

Cover and simmer over very low heat for 1 hour or until veal is tender. When veal is cooked there will be about 1/4 cup of liquid left. If not, uncover and cook over quick heat until the liquid is reduced.

Add sour cream and stir together to warm up. (Do not allow the cream to boil.)

Boil noodles and place on hot service platter. Pour creamed veal on top.

HEIDELBERG STEW

2 lb. stewing beef, cubed
2 tbsp. fat
1 can sauerkraut, drained
1/2 cup onion, chopped
3 cups sour cream (commercial)
  approximately

1/2 cup water
2 tsp. paprika
Salt and pepper (to taste)
1 tsp. monosodium glutamate

Brown meat slowly in fat.

Add sauerkraut, onion, 2 cups sour cream, water, paprika, salt, pepper and monosodium glutamate.

Cover and simmer for 2 hours, or until meat is tender, stirring often.

Just before serving, add about another cup of sour cream and taste for seasoning. (If mixture seems dry either before or after last addition of cream, add a bit more water.)

Serve with mashed or baked potatoes. (Serves 6.)

MOULDED POLISH PÂTÉ

1-2 lb. shoulder of pork	1 egg, well beaten
3 onions, quartered	1/4 tsp. nutmeg
1 bay leaf	1/2 tsp. marjoram
1/4 cup water	1 tsp. salt
1 lb. calf OR beef liver, unsliced	1/2 tsp. pepper
2 tbsp. butter	6 slices bacon

Place pork in a dripping pan with onions, bay leaf and water. Roast for 1 1/2 hours in a 400-degree oven.

Add to roasting pork (after 1 1/2 hours) calf or beef liver that has been spread with butter.

Continue cooking for half an hour, basting 3 or 4 times during cooking period. When done, set aside and cool.

Pass cooked meats through meat grinder twice.

Remove fat in dripping pan from juice by straining.

Pass cooked onions through strainer to make a purée and add to ground meat with juice strained from dripping pan.

Stir until well mixed and add egg, nutmeg, marjoram, salt and pepper.

Stir together until thoroughly blended (or use electric blender or food processor).

Line glass baking dish with raw bacon strips, arranging them in such a way that the ends hang over the top edge of the dish.

Pour in meat mixture and fold back hanging ends of bacon on top.

Place dish in a 400-degree oven for 30 minutes. Remove and cool to room temperature.

Set in refrigerator and serve very cold. (Serves 6.)

DANISH BRAISED HEART

1 heart (lamb, veal OR beef)	1 tsp. salt
1/4 cup bread crumbs	1/4 tsp. pepper
1 tbsp. fried bacon OR cooked ham	1 egg, slightly beaten
	3 to 5 tbsp. fat
1 tsp. dried parsley OR 1/4 tsp. basil	1 cup milk
	1 cup water OR 2 cups fresh or
Juice of 1/2 lemon	sour cream (commercial)

Wash heart with tepid water with a little vinegar added.

Mix bread crumbs, bacon or ham, parsley or basil, lemon juice and salt and pepper. Add egg. Stuff and sew heart to hold this dressing.

Roll in seasoned flour and brown in fat in a very heavy saucepan. When well browned, add milk and water or cream.

Cover and simmer for 40 minutes for lamb heart, 80 minutes for veal heart and 2 to 3 hours for beef heart. (Serves 4 to 6.)

HOPPING JOHN

An American recipe emigrated to Canadian tables.

2 cups dry peas	3 tbsp. bacon dripping
1/4 lb. salt pork	1 tsp. dry mustard
1 cup uncooked rice	1/2 cup minced celery leaves

Soak the peas overnight. Next morning, place in a saucepan with the salt pork and simmer until the peas are tender, from 1 1/2 to 2 hours.

Measure 3 cups of the water in which the peas were cooked and add to the rice with the bacon dripping, mustard and celery leaves.

Drain the peas and add to the rice mixture. Cook over slow fire for 1 hour.

Stir and serve with 2 or 3 slices of salt pork on top of each helping. (Serves 6.)

SHASHLYK

2-to-3-lb. beef tenderloin OR lamb from the loin or leg
1/2 cup wine vinegar
1/2 cup olive oil
2 or 3 cloves garlic, minced
1 tsp. salt
1/2 tsp. basil
1/4 tsp. thyme
2 medium-sized onions, sliced
Green peppers, cut into squares
Mushrooms

Cut meat into 2-inch squares.

Combine vinegar, oil, garlic, salt, basil and thyme and pour over meat.

Marinate from 5 to 7 hours.

Spear the meat on skewers with 1 slice of onion, 1 square of green pepper and 1 fresh mushroom between each piece of meat. (The vegetables and meat chosen are entirely a matter of individual taste. The Russian shashlyk is made without any vegetables between the meat.)

Cook by placing the meat in a dripping pan of a broiler, setting it 2 inches from the heat. Allow it to cook from 5 to 8 minutes depending on whether you prefer the meat rare or well done.

Serve with boiled rice, garnish with parsley and little heaps of shredded onions, minced green peppers and marinated tomatoes.

Note: The perfect way to cook shashlyk is over a wood or charcoal fire.

MADRAS CURRY

1 small onion
2 cloves garlic
4 tbsp. butter
1 tbsp. curry
1 2-to-3-lb. broiler
Chicken bouillon OR coconut milk OR fresh milk
Salt
Lime OR lemon juice

Chop onion and garlic finely and cook in butter till soft but not brown. Add 1 tablespoon (or more if desired) good curry and stir well over low heat 2 to 3 minutes.

Cut chicken into individual pieces (or have it cut by a butcher), place in pan and stir. Cook slowly for as long as possible without adding any moisture.

If curry gets dry, gradually add a little chicken bouillon or coconut milk to form a thickish gravy. When it is served there will be very little gravy — the curry taste is absorbed by the chicken.

Simmer slowly till chicken is tender and add salt and lime or lemon juice to taste, when ready to serve.

Serve with rice and condiments — mango chutney, ground cashews, grated coconut, green peppers, chopped pimiento, minced spring onions, Bombay duck (dried fish), lime or lemon slices. (Serves 4.)

SOUTH AFRICAN BOBOTIE

2 medium-sized onions, thinly sliced	1 lb. round steak or lamb, minced OR left-over meats
2 tbsp. shortening	1/2 cup dried apricots OR sultana raisins
4 tbsp. curry powder	
1 tbsp. sugar	1 cup bread crumbs
4 tbsp. water	2 eggs
2 tsp. salt	1 to 1 1/2 cups milk

Brown onions in shortening for a few minutes. Add curry powder, sugar and water. Cover and cook over low heat while preparing the following.

Place steak, lamb or left-over meats in an oven casserole and add salt. Chop apricots into small pieces and add to meat. Add bread crumbs.

Beat eggs with milk and pour into meat mixture, reserving 1/4 to pour over top. Mix well and flatten surface with a spoon. Arrange onion-curry on top or mix in, as desired.

Add remainder of egg mixture and place 4 dabs of butter on top. Bake in a 375-degree oven for three quarters of an hour, or until the top has a light brown crust.

Serve with boiled rice and a good chutney.

47

SUKIYAKI

There is much interest shown in Japanese food and I am adding a recipe for Sukiyaki. Like most Oriental food, Sukiyaki should be prepared just before eating.

2 tbsp. lard OR peanut oil
2 lb. tender beefsteak OR
    chicken, cut into shreds
2 onions, cut into shreds
3 shallots, cut on bias
1/2 cup mushrooms, cut into
    shreds
1 lb. spinach, shredded

1 cup bamboo shoots, cut into long
    sticks (optional)
1/2 cup soy sauce
2 tbsp. brown sugar
Monosodium glutamate (MSG)
1/4 cup sherry
5 or 6 cubes bean curds (optional)

Heat lard or peanut oil in a hot frying pan and add meat. Stir for about 5 minutes.

Remove to a meat dish and add onions, shallots, mushrooms, bamboo shoots, spinach, soy sauce and brown sugar to pan.

Sprinkle with monosodium glutamate and add sherry. Keep vegetables and mushrooms separated, the Japanese way, if you like, or mix together.

Cook for about 10 minutes, adding bean curds during last 5 minutes of cooking period just enough to heat them since they do not have to cook. If bean curds are not available, use any of the vegetables mentioned below.

Serve meat and vegetables with rice.

Note: Other vegetables that can be used in the Sukiyaki are leeks, onions, celery, Chinese cabbage, green peppers, shredded carrots, thin strips of turnips. Bean curds and bamboo shoots are delicious additions to Sukiyaki and are often obtainable in Chinese stores.

CHICKEN BROTH WITH EGG CUBES AND RICE

6 cups chicken stock
2 eggs
1/2 tsp. sugar
1 tsp. salt
1/4 tsp. pepper

1 or 2 green onions, chopped
  (use green ends, too)
1 tbsp. cooking oil
1 cup cooked rice

Heat chicken stock slowly. (Make stock from giblets, neck, wings and feet.)

Beat eggs, sugar, salt, pepper and onions together.

Heat oil in a very small frying pan. Turn egg mixture into pan and cook as you would for an omelet. When bottom is cooked turn omelet and cook the other side.

Allow to cool and cut into small squares.

Add rice to boiling stock, stir and pour into cups. Garnish with diced omelet. (Serves 4 to 6.)

CHINESE CABBAGE SOUP

2 tbsp. salad oil
1 tbsp. soy sauce
1 tsp. salt
1/2 tsp. pepper
1/2 lb. beef, cut into small
thin slices

6 cups water OR part water, part
consommé
3 cups Chinese cabbage, chopped
fine
2 green onions (whites and greens)

Mix salad oil, soy sauce, salt and pepper. Spread over beef which has been cut into very small, thin slices. Let stand in refrigerator 2 to 3 hours.

Bring water to a boil and when boiling hard add Chinese cabbage.

Stir and bring back to a boil, then add meat immediately. Bring back to a boil again, and add green onions which have been chopped finely.

Serve at once. (Serves 6.)

CHINESE FRIED RICE

3 tbsp. salad oil
1 egg
1/2 lb. fresh mushrooms
1/2 cup shallots (whites & greens)
1 small clove garlic

2 to 3 cups cooked rice
1/2 tsp. salt
1/4 tsp. pepper
2 tbsp. soy sauce
1/2 tsp. Monosodium glutamate
(MSG)

Heat salad oil in a large skillet. Break an egg into it and cook over very low heat. Remove from heat when well done and cut into shreds.

Slice fresh mushrooms and shallots thinly. Chop garlic finely. Have cooked rice, preferably cold, ready.

Add salt, pepper, soy sauce, monosodium glutamate, prepared vegetables, shredded egg and cooked rice to oil in skillet.

Stir together with a fork over medium heat for about 10 minutes or until rice is hot.

CHOP SUEY

1 lb. round beef, shoulder of pork OR veal	2 cups celery, chopped into 1-inch pieces
3 tbsp. soy sauce	1 cup green pepper
1 tbsp. dark brown sugar	1/2 lb. fresh mushrooms
4 tbsp. salad oil	1 cup cold water
3 onions, chopped	2 tbsp. cornstarch
2 to 3 cloves minced garlic	Salt and pepper (to taste)

1/2 to 1 lb. chop suey OR bean sprouts

Cut beef, pork or veal into very thin slices, cutting against the grain of the meat. Combine soy sauce and dark brown sugar together and add sliced meat. Stir together and let stand 15 to 20 minutes.

Heat salad oil and fry in it chopped onions, minced garlic, and when lightly browned add meat. Stir, cover and cook for exactly 8 minutes over medium heat.

Chop celery, green pepper and fresh mushrooms into 1-inch pieces. Add to meat mixture after the 8 minutes of cooking. Stir together.

Add cold water mixed with cornstarch, salt and pepper to taste. Add chop suey or bean sprouts. Stir together, cover and cook for 5 minutes. (Serves 3 to 4.)

EGG ROLLS

DOUGH

2 cups flour, sifted
2 tbsp. cornstarch
1 tsp. salt
1 egg, beaten
1 tsp. sugar

4 cups water
Oil for pan OR griddle
1 tbsp. flour mixed with 2 tbsp. water

Sift flour, cornstarch and salt together. Beat in eggs and sugar and gradually beat in enough water to make a smooth, thin batter.

Rub a 6-inch pan or small griddle lightly with oil, and set over low heat. (A crepe pan is fine.)

Beat batter and pour about 4 tablespoons into the centre of the pan.

Tilt the pan to spread batter over entire surface. This makes a very thin pancake. Pour off excess batter, if any. As soon as the cake shrinks away from the sides of the pan, use your fingers to pick it up quickly at one side and carefully turn it over.

Let it cook on other side, then remove from pan and place on a plate.

To roll, lay the cooked paste or pancake on a table or large plate and place 3 or 4 tablespoons of filling (recipe follows) on each. Spread filling lengthwise.

Fold the pastry edge which is along the length of the filling over the filling, then fold one end over this, then the other end and finally moisten the edge of the remaining side with flour mixed with water. Fold this over the roll and press lightly together. (Both filling and egg-roll skin should be completely cold before the roll is made. It will tear easily if still warm.)

To fry, heat about 2 inches of cooking oil in a deep 10-inch skillet or wok. When hot, place the rolls carefully in the skillet and fry until golden brown on all sides.

Lift out, drain, and serve hot with English mustard or a mustard sauce and plum sauce. (Serves 8.)

FILLING

1/2 cup celery, minced
1 cup cabbage, finely shredded
1/2 cup boiling water
2 tbsp. cooking oil
1/2 cup cooked or canned shrimp
  diced
1 tsp. salt

1/2 cup roast pork, ham OR beef
  diced (optional)
2 green onions, minced (use green
  ends too)
1/2 tsp. pepper
3 tbsp. soy sauce

Place celery and cabbage in boiling water. Cover and cook till tender.

Drain immediately and roll in a clean towel. Press well to remove as much moisture as possible.

Heat oil in a frying pan and cook shrimp and meat from 2 to 3 minutes. Stir.

Add celery, cabbage, onions, salt, pepper and soy sauce. Stir until delicately golden all over. Allow to cool.

Fill pancakes as described.

CHINESE PORK AND RICE

2 tbsp. butter OR salad oil
1 cup uncooked rice
1 large onion, thinly sliced
1/2 tsp. salt
1 bouillon cube
1 1/2 cups boiling water

2 stalks celery, cut into 1-inch
   pieces
1 green pepper, cut into 1-inch
   pieces
1 cup cooked pork, diced
2 tsp. soy sauce

Heat butter or salad oil in a heavy frying pan.

Add uncooked rice and onion.

Season with salt and cook over medium heat until rice grains turn golden brown, stirring occasionally.

Add bouillon cube to water, dissolve and pour on rice.

Cover pan and cook for 20 minutes over low heat or until rice is tender.   Do not overcook.

Meanwhile, cut celery, pepper and pork into small pieces.

Add celery, green pepper and pork when rice is cooked.

Cover tightly and place over very low heat for about 10 minutes, or until vegetables are tender but still slightly crisp.

Stir in soy sauce when ready to serve.   (Serves 4.)

ORIENTAL PORK

1/2 cup soy sauce
3 tbsp. sugar
2 green onions, chopped
2 cloves garlic, minced
1/2 tsp. pepper

1/2 tsp. powdered ginger
1 tbsp. sesame seeds (optional)
2 lb. pork tenderloin
1 tbsp. peanut oil

Combine soy sauce, sugar, onions, garlic, pepper, ginger and sesame seeds in a bowl and stir.

Slice pork into 1/4-inch slices or have the butcher do it.

Marinate in soy-sauce mixture for 2 or 3 hours.   Stir pork frequently.   Remove from the marinade and place it on a broiling pan which has been oiled lightly with peanut oil.

Broil, with oven door partly open, for about 10 minutes, turning once.   While meat is cooking, heat soy-sauce marinade and serve hot in a sauce boat.

Meat may be cooked in a frying pan if cooked slowly. (Serves 6.)

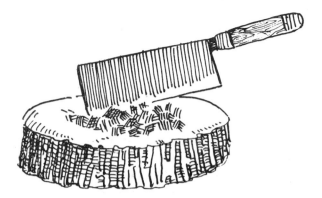

SWEET AND PUNGENT PORK

1 egg
1/2 cup flour
1/2 tsp. salt
3 or 4 tbsp. water
1 lb. pork shoulder, cut into
    large cubes
Oil for deep frying
1 cup canned pineapple cubes

1 green pepper, cut diagonally in
    about 1-inch-wide pieces
1/2 cup vinegar
1/4 cup brown sugar
1 cup water
1 tbsp. molasses
1 tomato, cut into 4 to 6 pieces
2 tbsp. cornstarch

Make a thin batter by beating the egg, then mixing flour, salt and 3 or 4 tbsp. water with it.

Pour over pork, mix to coat the pieces, then fry them, piece by piece in deep, hot oil until brown.   Drain.

Mix pineapple, green pepper, vinegar, brown sugar, 3/4 cup water and molasses.   Stir until it boils; add tomato.

Mix cornstarch with remaining 1/4 cup of water and stir into the sauce.

Cook until thickened; add pork, stir to mix well and serve at once.   (Serves 4.)

CANTONESE DUCK

2 tbsp. soy sauce
1 tbsp. sherry
1 shallot, chopped
Breast and legs of duck
2 eggs

4 tbsp. cornstarch
1/2 tsp. salt
4 tbsp. water
3 tbsp. lard OR vegetable oil

Mix in a bowl soy sauce, sherry and shallot.
Add breast and leg of duck and let marinate 1 hour.
Mix eggs, cornstarch, salt and water together in a paste.
Roll pieces of duck in mixture.
Heat lard or vegetable oil in large skillet.
Fry duck 2 minutes on each side.   Turn several times and fry 10 minutes or until skin becomes crisp.
Cut duck in half-inch slices, and serve with a little bowl of 3 tbsp. salt and 1/2 tsp. pepper mixed together.

CHINESE FRIED SHRIMPS

1 egg, beaten	1/2 cup salad oil
2 tbsp. flour	2/3 cup minced onion
1/2 tsp. salt	1 tbsp. cornstarch
Dash of pepper	1 tsp. soy sauce
1 lb. shelled, cleaned raw shrimps (thaw, if frozen)	3/4 cup chicken bouillon

Combine egg with flour, salt and pepper. Add shrimps and stir till coated.

Heat salad oil till very hot, add shrimps, one by one, and fry until golden (about 6 to 7 minutes). Drain on paper towelling and keep hot on warm platter.

When shrimps are cooked, remove all but 2 tbsp. of oil from skillet, sauté onion in this and add combined cornstarch, soy sauce and bouillon. Stir till thickened.

Pour over hot, boiled rice on platter and serve. (Serves 2 to 3.)

A good accompaniment is a salad of grapefruit, apple and green pepper, a light dessert and tea.

SWEET AND SOUR SHRIMP

1 lb. cooked shrimp, fresh, frozen or canned	1/4 cup vinegar
	1 tbsp. soy sauce
1/4 cup brown sugar	1 No. 2 can pineapple chunks
2 tbsp. cornstarch	1 green pepper, cut into strips
1/2 tsp. salt	2 small onions, cut into rings

Remove veins and shell from shrimp.

Mix in a saucepan brown sugar, cornstarch, salt, vinegar, soy sauce and juice drained from canned pineapple.

Cook until slightly thick, stirring constantly.

Add green pepper, onions and pineapple chunks. Cook 2 or 3 minutes.

Remove from heat, add shrimp and let stand about 10 minutes.

Just before serving bring to a boil, stirring constantly.

Serve with hot rice or noodles. (Serves 3 or 4.)

SWEET AND SOUR MEAT BALLS

3 large green peppers
1 lb. ground beef
1 egg
2 tbsp. flour
1 1/2 tsp. salt
1/8 tsp. pepper
3/4 cup oil OR fat

1/3 cup chicken bouillon
1 small can pineapple chunks,
    drained
3 tbsp. cornstarch
2 tsp. soy sauce
1/2 cup vinegar
1/2 cup honey
2/3 cup chicken bouillon

Cut each pepper into 6 pieces, removing seeds and membrane, and cook uncovered in boiling water until almost tender.   Set aside.

Form ground beef, seasoned to taste, into 16 small balls.

Make a batter by beating together egg, flour, 1/2 tsp. salt and a dash of pepper.

Dip meat balls into batter and place on a plate.

Put oil or fat and 1 tsp. salt in a preheated, heavy 10-inch frying pan or a wok.

Place meat balls in pan and brown over moderate heat until golden brown on one side (about 5 minutes).

Turn meat balls over and brown on other side.

Remove to a hot platter and keep warm.

Pour out all but 1 tbsp. of oil from pan.

Add 1/3 cup of chicken bouillon, pineapple and green pepper and cook over a very low flame for about 10 minutes.

Blend together and add cornstarch, soy sauce, vinegar, honey and 2/3 cup chicken bouillon.   Stir constantly until juice thickens and mixture is very hot (about 5 minutes).

Pour over meat balls and serve immediately with hot, boiled rice.   (Serves 4.)

Stir a hint of soy sauce into chicken stock, and you have a Chinese flavour.

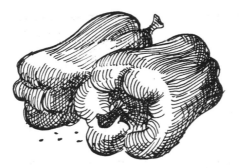

CHINESE CHICKEN LIVERS AND GREEN PEPPERS

Chicken livers (as many as desired)
2 tbsp. soy sauce
1 tbsp. honey OR brown sugar
1 small onion, chopped finely
2 to 3 tbsp. consommé OR water
3 tbsp. salad oil
2 to 3 onions

2, 3 or 4 green peppers (as many
   or as few as you like)
1 clove garlic, chopped finely
1 tbsp. cornstarch
1/4 cup water
Salt and pepper (to taste)

Combine soy sauce, honey or brown sugar, 1 onion and consommé or water, and place livers (wash and dry them first) in the mixture. Marinate for half an hour.

Heat oil in a frying pan or wok until hot, but not smoking. Add livers together with liquid, stir and cover. Cook over low heat for 5 minutes.

Cut green peppers and remaining onions into long thin slices (Chinese fashion). Chop garlic finely or crush.

Mix cornstarch in a cup with water.

Add green peppers, onions and garlic to liver mixture in frying pan. Pour over cornstarch and water, stir and let mixture come to a boil. Stir again, cover and cook for 5 minutes (no longer). The vegetables should be crisp when you eat them. Add salt and pepper.

Serve with rice. Chinese food shouldn't sit around waiting, so do not cook this dish until about half an hour before the meal.

BARBECUED GARLIC SPARERIBS

4 tbsp. white sugar
1 tbsp. salt
4 tbsp. honey
3 tsp. soy sauce

3 tbsp. consomme´
2 lb. pork spareribs, cut into
  individual pieces
3 to 4 cloves garlic, thinly sliced

Mix sugar, salt, honey, soy sauce and consommé in a bowl.
Cut spareribs into individual pieces. Place in sugar and soy mixture, and roll around to coat each piece. Cover top with garlic. Cover bowl and let stand in refrigerator 12 to 24 hours.

To cook, place pieces of spareribs on grill of oven rack. Place slices of garlic here and there over the meat. Cook for 30 minutes in a 400-degree oven. Turn and cook another 30 minutes, lowering the heat to 350 degrees if browning too fast. (Serves 6.)

PINEAPPLE SPARERIBS

2 qts. water
1/2 cup vinegar
4 lb. spareribs (cut into 2-inch
  pieces)

1/2 cup cornstarch
1/4 cup soy sauce
1/4 cup dark molasses

Heat water to boiling point and add vinegar. Add ribs, cover till water begins to boil again; uncover, simmer for 15 minutes. Drain and cool. May be done a day in advance.

Mix cornstarch, soy sauce and molasses in a large bowl, and allow ribs to soak in mixture until each is well coated. Most of the liquid will be absorbed.

Fry ribs in hot fat (370 degrees) until brown. Keep fat very hot while cooking. Fry a few ribs at a time. Set aside until ready to glaze (see below). (Serves 6 to 8.)

GLAZE

1/2 cup sugar
3/4 cup water
3/4 cup vinegar
3/4 cup pineapple syrup

1 can pineapple slices, chopped
  into 1-inch pieces
1 1/2 green peppers, cut into 1-inch
  cubes

Combine ingredients, with exception of peppers and pineapple, in a large pan. Heat to boiling. Add meat to hot syrup, cover and simmer 30 minutes until meat is glazed and tender. Add peppers and pineapple. Serve with boiled rice.

CHINESE BARBECUED SPARERIBS

3 lb. fresh pork spareribs	1 1/2 tsp. salt
1 1/2 cups soy sauce	2 tbsp. sugar OR honey
2 cloves crushed garlic	1 tbsp. sherry

Have your butcher chop spareribs into 1-inch pieces for easy eating.

Wash ribs and remove gristle. Dry on a towel.

Combine ribs with remaining ingredients. Make certain ribs are coated with sauce and allow them to soak for half an hour.

Place ribs on broiler and broil until they are brown on all sides. Or, if you prefer, brown them on top of the stove, then place them in a 350-degree oven. They should be well done in about an hour, but don't let them burn.

(Serves 4 to 6.)

CHINESE SWEET 'N SOUR SPARERIBS

Spareribs

4 tbsp. sugar

1 tbsp. salt

4 tbsp. honey

2 tbsp. soy sauce

3 tbsp. consommé

3 tbsp. salad oil

2 tbsp. sherry

2 slices green ginger

   OR 1/4 tsp. powdered ginger

1 tsp. soy sauce

1 tomato, peeled and diced

1 tbsp. cornstarch

1/4 cup water

Marinate spareribs, which have been chopped into bite-size pieces by your butcher, in a mixture of sugar, salt, honey, 2 tbsp. soy sauce and consommé. Leave ribs in this liquid for 8 to 12 hours in the refrigerator.

Drain (retain liquid) spareribs.

Melt salad oil in pan (your electric frying pan or wok) and add spareribs and brown quickly over medium heat.

Add 3 tbsp. of sauce in which ribs have been marinated, sherry and ginger, 1 tsp. soy sauce, tomato, peeled and diced.

Stir, cover and simmer for 20 to 25 minutes.

When ribs are cooked, mix cornstarch in water and add. Stir till sauce is transparent. (Left-over marinating sauce may be kept in refrigerator till you do ribs again.)

Serve with rice.

ALMOND COOKIES

1 cup rice flour

1/2 cup brown sugar

2 cups blanched, ground almonds

1/3 cup butter

Sift together rice flour and brown sugar. Add almonds.

Cream butter and work smoothly into flour-sugar mixture. Add a few drops of water if required to hold the dough together.

Shape into small balls and place on a greased cookie sheet, leaving 1 inch between each cookie. Press almonds on top.

Bake in a 350-degree oven for 15 minutes. (Makes 24 to 36.)

Part 1

Beginnings

Appetizers

Appetizers have a different meaning to Canadians and Americans than to cooks in France. We have developed a dubious style of entertaining where, sometimes, the only nourishment served consists of finger-food eaten with a strong drink. Cocktail parties are not my idea of fun although I know they are a good way to entertain a crowd without serving them dinner. If appetizers precede a dinner they should serve only to stimulate the appetite but they should reasonably fortify the guest who is driving from your party to dinner elsewhere. I feel a responsibility about serving alcohol to guests who drive cars. I rely on home-made pâté as the pièce de résistance and notice that most people love it. The French trick of marinating meats and vegetables in vinaigrette is one I've used for years — so many small bits and pieces can be the base for a delicious plate of hors d'oeuvres which can also be served as a light meal.

ONION PIE

This is one of those dishes which gain a reputation for a cook. It is the extra dish, the unexpected treat which can even be eaten with a salad, as a main course.

PASTRY	FILLING
1 1/2 cups flour	2 tbsp. butter
2 tsp. baking powder	5 to 6 medium onions, chopped
1/2 tsp. salt	2 eggs, beaten
1/3 cup plus 1 tbsp. lard	1/4 tsp. nutmeg
Milk	1 cup sour cream (commercial)
	Salt and pepper

Mix pastry (or use a biscuit mix following directions for pie pastry on box).

Sift flour, baking powder and salt, cut in lard and add just enough milk so dough can be rolled.

Fit pastry into a pie plate, prick with fork. Refrigerate.

Meanwhile, melt butter and sauté onions till they are soft and golden. · Do not brown them.

Combine eggs, nutmeg and sour cream.

Place onions in pie shell, sprinkle with salt and pepper and pour egg mixture over them.

Place in a 400-degree oven for 7 minutes, reduce heat to 300 and bake an additional 15 minutes or until a knife, inserted in the filling, comes out clean as with a custard.
Serves 4-6.

SALAMI SLICES

1 pkg. cream cheese	1 tbsp. chives, chopped
1/2 tsp. dry mustard	OR green onions
1/2 tsp. salt	1 lb. salami, thinly sliced
1 garlic clove, grated	Chopped parsley

Blend cheese, mustard, salt, garlic and chives or onions.

Spread one half of mixture on one third of salami slices, top with another slice, spread mixture and place third salami slice on top.

Cut salami into 4 wedges, dip edges in a saucer of finely chopped parsley and keep covered in refrigerator.

PIQUANT NUTS

1 tbsp. butter OR margarine	Garlic salt
1 tbsp. soy sauce	Celery salt
2 cups filbert meats or other nuts	Monosodium glutamate
Onion salt	

Melt butter or margarine in a shallow baking pan.
Stir in soy sauce. Add filbert meats and mix well.
Sprinkle generously with onion salt, garlic salt, celery salt
and monosodium glutamate. Mix again.
Bake in a 350-degree oven for 15 to 20 minutes, until nuts
are nicely browned, stirring several times.
Cool before serving.

STUFFED EGGS

12 eggs	3 tbsp. parsley, chopped
1/4 cup mayonnaise	Capers
3 tbsp. onion, grated	Stuffed olives, sliced
3 anchovy fillets, chopped (optional)	

Cook eggs until hard. Shell and cut into halves.
Remove yolks very carefully and chill whites.
Add mayonnaise, onion, anchovy, parsley and a few
capers to the yolks and blend well.
Fill the white shells and top each with sliced stuffed
olives.
Wrap in foil or wax-paper and place in empty egg
cartons. This will make handling easier if they are being
taken to a picnic.

Variation: For each 4 yolks, combine 2 tbsp. blue cheese,
1 tsp. prepared mustard, pinch of dehydrated horseradish or
the prepared variety, 1 tsp. finely chopped chives or green
onions, pinch of thyme and salt and pepper. Blend with
yolks and stuff eggs.

*If nuts become stale, put them in a moderate oven for
ten to fifteen minutes to freshen them.*

PICKLED EGGS

8 fresh eggs, hard-boiled	1 tsp. whole allspice
1 qt. white vinegar	1/2 tsp. mace
1 tbsp. grated ginger root	2-inch cinnamon stick
8 whole cloves	1/2 tsp. salt

Hard cook the eggs (about 20 minutes) and place in a bowl of cold water. Cool and remove shells, taking care not to injure the smooth white surface. (Older eggs peel better than fresh ones.)

Pack eggs into a large-mouth covered jar. Tie all the spices into a cheesecloth bag and place in a covered pot along with the vinegar. Bring to a boil slowly. Boil for 5 minutes. Remove from stove, and leave the spice bag in the vinegar while it cools for two hours. Strain.

Cover the eggs with spiced vinegar and add the 1/2 tsp. salt, and reserve remaining vinegar for other pickling.

Cover tightly. The eggs will keep for four months and are at their best about two months after they are made.

Store in the refrigerator if possible or on a cool shelf.

CHOPPED LIVER

1 lb. liver, trimmed
2 hard-boiled eggs
1 onion

Salt and pepper (to taste)
2 tbsp. butter OR chicken fat

Drop liver into rapidly boiling water and cook gently until well done (10 to 15 minutes).

Remove from water and cool.

Put liver, eggs and onion through a food grinder, using the fine blade.

Season with salt and pepper and add butter or chicken fat, working it through the liver with a fork. (The liver should be moist enough to hold together.) Add more butter if necessary.

Spread on dry toast cut in assorted shapes, or on crackers.

DANISH FOIE GRAS

This makes a delicious spread for biscuits. It is a fine addition to the buffet table.

1 lb. veal OR beef liver
1/4 cup onions, chopped
1/2 lb. minced fresh pork
2 eggs
2 cups table cream

1 tsp. pepper
3 tsp. salt
1 1/4 cups all-purpose flour
3 bay leaves

Chop liver finely and fry onions in butter or oil.

Mix first eight ingredients in a bowl.

Cream or blend well.

Turn it into a well-buttered mould. Arrange bay leaves over top. Cover.

Place mould in a pan containing hot water and bake in a 350-degree oven for 2 hours. Uncover mould at the end of one hour and bake uncovered for the remainder of the time.

MUSHROOM LIVER SPREAD

4 chicken livers	2 tsp. chives, chopped
1 clove of garlic	2 tsp. sherry
3 tbsp. butter	1/2 tsp. salt
1/2 lb. mushrooms, stems removed	Pinch of pepper

Sauté chicken livers and garlic in 2 tbsp. butter until livers are cooked.

Discard garlic.   Remove livers and chop finely.

Slice mushrooms and add with 1 tbsp. butter to pan in which livers were cooked.

Sauté about 6 minutes.

Finely chop and combine with chopped livers, chives, sherry, salt and pepper.

Blend until smooth.

Use as a spread on Melba toast.   (Makes 2/3 cup.)

MUSHROOM APPETIZERS

3 tbsp. butter	1 tsp. paprika
1/2 lb. mushrooms, chopped finely	2 hard-cooked egg yolks, chopped
1 tsp. salt	2 tsp. lemon juice
1/4 tsp. pepper	2 tsp. grated cheese

Melt butter in a skillet and sauté the mushrooms for 10 minutes.

Drain, if any liquid remains.

Add salt, pepper, paprika, egg yolks, lemon juice and cheese.   Mix well.

Pile on buttered toast rounds and place under the broiler for 1 minute.   (Makes 18 canapés.)

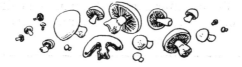

FAVOURITE MUSHROOM CANAPÉS

These are a filling accompaniment to a before-dinner drink and I have served them, along with olives, as the main item on the hors-d'oeuvres tray.

1/2 lb. fresh mushrooms	Salt and pepper
French dressing	1 thin French loaf
1 tsp. curry powder	OR Melba rounds

Break off mushroom caps and slice thinly.   Slice stems and chop into small pieces.

Make a good French dressing (2 parts oil to one part wine vinegar) and shake vigorously.

Add curry powder and season to taste.

Pour dressing over mushrooms in a bowl and marinate for at least half an hour.

Meanwhile, slice crusty bread very thinly and spread with butter.   Canapés should be bite size.   If Melba toast is used, butter lightly.

With a spatula, arrange drained mushrooms on slices. Dressing may be reserved for use in salads.

Serve in a shallow basket or on a platter. (Serves 10.)

BEEF BITES

1 lb. ground steak	1/2 tsp. dry mustard
1 tbsp. steak sauce	1 tbsp. chopped parsley
1 clove garlic, minced	1 tsp. black pepper
1 tsp. salt	3 tbsp. butter
1/4 lb. grated Cheddar cheese	2 tbsp. oil

Combine all ingredients except butter and shape into very small balls.

Cook quickly in butter and oil, browning on all sides.

Drain on paper towelling and keep hot.   Serve on toothpicks.

To store parsley, wash it thoroughly, drain well and place in a tightly covered container in the refrigerator.

HOT CHEESE BITES

4 tbsp. butter
1/2 cup flour

1 6-oz. pkg. any sharp cheese

Cream butter and cheese, add flour and blend well. Chill.
Roll into small balls, place on ungreased cookie sheet, press down with a fork, and bake at 400 degrees for 6-8 minutes.
Serve hot. Dough may be prepared several days in advance and stored in refrigerator.

PÂTÉ BALLS

1 pkg. (3 oz.) cream cheese
1 tin pâté OR devilled ham

1/2 tsp. curry
Chopped walnuts

Mix together cream cheese, pâté or devilled ham and curry. Place in refrigerator for 3 hours.
Shape into small balls and roll each ball in chopped walnuts. Keep in refrigerator until ready to serve.

STUFFED HAM À LA PARMA

I am often asked for suggestions for midnight snacks, a habit still enjoyed in Canadian homes. This is an idea I favour because it is simple and not too heavy.

2 to 3 oz. cream cheese
3 tbsp. table cream OR whole
   milk
1/2 cup nuts, finely minced

1 tbsp. prepared mustard
   OR 1 tsp. curry powder
Celery hearts
Ham slices

Cream until light and fluffy cream cheese, table cream or milk, nuts, prepared mustard or curry powder.
Prepare as many small hearts of celery as there are slices of ham.
Spread slices of ham with a good coating of cheese mixture.
Place a celery heart on each and roll up. Cover and keep refrigerated until ready to serve as an evening snack after bridge or poker.

SPREAD-YOUR-OWN MIXTURES

These are all mixed the same way.   Place ingredients in a bowl and work with spoon until smooth and creamy.   Or better still, combine them with your food processor or blender.

SHALLOT MIXTURE
1 3-oz. pkg. cream cheese   1/4 cup minced nuts
2 tbsp. butter   Pinch of ground anise seed
1 shallot, chopped finely

OLIVE MIXTURE
1 3-oz. pkg. cream cheese   1 small tin chopped black or
2 tbsp. butter   green olives
Salt to taste

SARDINE MIXTURE
1 tin sardines with oil   1 tsp. curry powder
4 tbsp. butter   1/4 tsp. salt

HERB BREAD

Garlic bread is something everyone knows about but the idea of using chopped green onions and herbs may be new to many.

1 loaf French bread   Pinch of dried tarragon OR basil
1/4 cup butter   OR parsley
1/2 cup chopped green onions

Slice bread.
Combine butter, herbs and onions and spread on slices.
Rearrange loaf, wrap in foil, leaving a narrow slit on top.
Place in a 350-degree oven for 15 minutes, or till crisp
and hot.
Serve piping hot in a basket.
Loaf may be prepared and frozen before heating.   I have
done as many as 12 at one time and find this a time saver
when I'm having a party.

HERB BUTTER

The difference between a slab of butter and a mound of this fragrant butter is too obvious to mention. The latter does wonders for a plain slice of bread.

1/2 cup butter	1/4 tsp. thyme
1/4 tsp. basil	1/2 tsp. lemon juice
1/4 tsp. marjoram	

Blend together and use on hot bread or rolls and on cooked green vegetables, baked or fried fish, fried chicken. Use one or all herbs at one time.

HERB BISCUITS

Biscuit mix	Basil, tarragon, savory OR any favourite herb

Follow package directions for making biscuits and add crushed fresh or dried herbs to the dry mix before adding liquid.

Bake as directed and serve hot, generously spread with butter.

TUNA PÂTÉ

Having the kitchen shop has increased my collection of recipes — our customers are cooking enthusiasts and the conversation is always about food. Patsy Stephenson passed on this one which I turn out in the food processor in 30 seconds. It keeps well in the fridge.

1 8-oz. can quality tuna fish	Lots of black pepper, coarsely ground
2 tbsp. mayonnaise	
4 oz. salted butter	Lemon juice, to taste

Drain oil from can. Heat butter and combine with other ingredients in blender or food processor. Blend till very smooth — it will be rather runny. Pour into crock or serving bowl and refrigerate for at least 24 hours. Spread on crackers. (Makes eight ounces.)

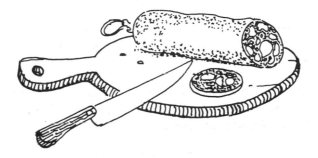

VEAL AND HAM PÂTÉ

1 1/2 lb. veal, finely ground	Pinch of rosemary OR marjoram
1 1/2 lb. ground pork	Pinch of nutmeg
2 cloves garlic, finely chopped	2 eggs
1 cup undiluted consommé	Thin strips of salt pork
1 tsp. salt	Cooked ham, sliced paper thin
1 tsp. pepper	4 tbsp. green onions, chopped
1 tsp. basil	4 tbsp. parsley, chopped

Combine veal, pork, garlic, 1/2 cup undiluted consommé, salt, pepper, basil, rosemary or marjoram, nutmeg and eggs.

Line a large casserole with thin strips of salt pork. Add a layer of meat mixture, then a layer of cooked ham and a generous sprinkling of the mixed onions and parsley.

Repeat the layers until the casserole is filled, ending with the ground mixture at the top.

Press down well and add remaining 1/2 cup of undiluted consommé.

Cover with more thin strips of salt pork and bake, covered, for 2 1/2 hours at 325 degrees.

Remove the cover and weight the pâté down while it cools.

Recover and chill before serving. (Serves 12 to 14.)

PÂTÉ MAISON

1 lb. ground lean pork
1/2 lb. ground fat salt pork
1 lb. pork liver, chopped
2 cloves garlic, finely chopped
(optional)
6 green onions, finely chopped
1 tsp. salt

1 tsp. pepper
Pinch of nutmeg
1/2 tsp. thyme
3 eggs, beaten
Bacon stips OR salt pork
1 cup Canadian white wine
OR apple juice

Combine ground pork, salt pork, pork liver, garlic, green onions, salt, pepper, nutmeg, thyme and beaten eggs and blend together thoroughly.

Line a round or oblong casserole with strips of bacon or salt pork.

Add the meat mixture, well packed down, and pour white wine or apple juice over it.

Press down again and top with additional strips of bacon or salt pork.

Cover and bake for 2 hours at 325 degrees until thoroughly cooked. Set the casserole in another pan as it may boil over.

Remove from the oven when done, uncover and weight the pâté down so that it will have a better texture.

Cool and remove weight, then chill before serving. There will be a thin film of fat on and around the pâté. Leave this on, since it will preserve it. (Serves 12 to 14.)

Soups

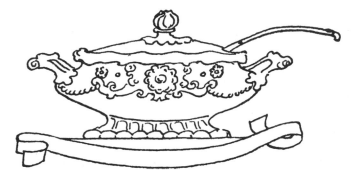

Soup, like stew, is a basic food in Canadian homes from fall to spring. Filling and healthy, it warms us after school or work, or after we've been skiing or shovelling snow.

I've always been a soup maker. I am an extravagant but not a wasteful cook and I can't bring myself to throw away any food that can be added to soup. When I had no children my freezer stored quantities of stock that took a long time to use up. Today, soup rarely makes it to the freezer. My kids come in from school in winter and eat a bowl of soup with cheese sprinkled over it as a snack. Our family favourite is potato and leek soup — which we eat hot or cold depending on the season — so I make sure that in the fall I cache away a supply of sautéed leeks.

The first requirement for soup making is the stock pot. The pot should be capacious, tall and narrow. A wide Dutch Oven isn't as effective although it can certainly be used if you have nothing else. A stock pot is a good investment because it can be used for preserves, for cooking spaghetti, corn-on-the-cob, potatoes or lobster and for any quantity cooking.

A freezer induces you to plan for soup. Whenever you have meat trimmings, bones, tired celery and carrots, tops of vegetables, leek greens and you're not in the mood for stock making, put them into a plastic bag and freeze. The frozen contents can be put directly into a roasting pan and roasted at 400 degrees until everything is browned. Then scrape the pan into the stock pot, cover with water, add thyme, parsley, pepper, bay leaf and some fresh celery, carrots, onions and leeks, if you have them, and cook up the base for marvellous gravies and sauces as well as fabulous soups. In spite of our accelerated living, the making of stock isn't a thing of the past — and it doesn't allow you to waste.

If you own a blender or food processor you can turn left-over vegetables into great soups in seconds. Canned, frozen and dehydrated soups also fit into my daily cooking.

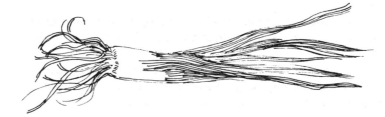

Add a swirl of sour cream to a cup of hot or cold soup.

VICHYSSOISE

This is our favourite family soup — hot or cold, and topped with chives from the garden. My kids never balked at drinking cold soup. Nor can you ever go wrong serving this soup to knowledgeable eaters; leeks are the aristocrats of the onion family and make any dish memorable.

1 cup onions, chopped (optional)	1 qt. chicken stock or more
2 leeks, chopped (the white part only)	Salt (to taste)
	1/4 tsp. white pepper
1/4 cup melted butter	1 cup light cream
2 cups raw potatoes, diced	2 tbsp. chives, chopped

Sauté onions and leeks in butter until they are soft and yellow (about 20 minutes).   Do not brown them.

Add potatoes and pour in the chicken stock.

Add salt to taste (depending upon how salty the stock is) and white pepper.

Cook for about 20-30 minutes, or until potatoes are soft.   Put through a fine sieve, food mill or food processor while hot.

Return soup to stove after sieving it, heat to boiling, remove from the fire and add cream.   Heat again but *do not boil.*

Pour into a hot tureen and sprinkle chives on top.

For cold vichyssoise, chill soup thoroughly before adding the cream.   (Makes about 2 quarts.)

Note: You can freeze the leek base for vichyssoise. The leeks are sliced, sautéed in butter for 5 minutes, then poured, butter and all, into a plastic bag to be chilled and frozen. When ready to use, remove leeks from freezer, thaw or place immediately in pan with hot chicken stock and remaining ingredients.

> *Finely chopped parsley and a slice of lemon are musts for plain soups.*

COCK-A-LEEKIE

Another main-course soup which the Scots invented and we make far too infrequently in Canadian homes. Many an old bird comes out of this soup tasting like a young chick.

1 boiling fowl OR 1 chicken 3 to 4 lb.	1 tsp. thyme
3 qts. water	1 bay leaf
3 to 4 onions, sliced	Salt and pepper
1 tbsp. chopped parsley	1 bunch leeks (6 to 12)
	6 potatoes OR 1/2 cup uncooked rice

Cut chicken into pieces. Place in a large saucepan or soup kettle and cover with boiling water.

Add onions, parsley, thyme, bay leaf, salt and pepper.

Cover and simmer until the meat is ready to fall from bones. (A young bird cooks in about an hour, a fowl will probably take about 2 hours.)

Remove chicken and add leeks to the stock (cut into pieces an inch long — both the green and white parts of the leeks can be used).

Add potatoes, peeled and diced, or well-washed rice. Turn up heat and cook briskly about 20 minutes until potatoes or rice are tender.

Meanwhile, remove skin and bones from cooked chicken and cut meat into good-sized pieces.

Before serving, add meat to soup and taste for seasoning. (Serves 6 to 8.) This is a main-course soup and needs a spoon and fork.

MINESTRONE

1 lb. beef with bone	1/8 tsp. pepper
3 1/2 qts. cold water	1 cup cut-up green beans
2 tbsp. salt	3/4 cup diced celery
1 cup dried kidney beans	2/3 cup shelled peas (optional)
2 peeled cloves garlic	2 cups finely shredded cabbage
1 tbsp. olive OR salad oil	1 cup diced, pared carrots
1/2 cup minced onion	1 cup canned tomatoes
1/2 cup minced parsley	1/2 cup spaghetti, broken up finely
1 tbsp. salt	Grated Parmesan cheese

Place beef in kettle. Add water, 2 tbsp. salt and washed kidney beans. Cover and bring to a boil. Skim, re-cover and simmer for 4 hours.

Brown garlic in oil, discard garlic, then sauté onion and parsley in same oil until onion is tender, but not brown.

Remove bone and meat from stock. Add onion, parsley and remaining ingredients except spaghetti and cheese.

Cover and simmer 30 minutes. Add spaghetti and cook for 10 minutes.

Serve with a bowl of cheese to be sprinkled on top.

FRENCH ONION SOUP

This recipe is a life saver to anyone who wants an easy beginning to a meal. It has the added attraction of being a soup most people enjoy. Like most soups and stews it is better to let it sit for a day in the refrigerator to allow flavours to blend. It can be the main course for lunch or supper in which case I always prepare for seconds.

1/3 cup butter	3 cans beef consommé, diluted
5 large onions, thinly sliced	OR
1/2 tsp. pepper	3 bouillon cubes and water
1 cup grated Swiss cheese	4-6 slices French bread

Melt butter, add onions and stir well.

Cover and simmer for 20 minutes, just till edges of onions are browned lightly.

Add consommé or bouillon cubes dissolved in 6 cups of hot water.

Cover and simmer half an hour. Taste for seasoning.

Serve with thick slices of French bread which have been generously sprinkled with grated cheese.

Place slices in a very hot oven or under broiler until cheese is soft and toast is brown. Place a slice in the bottom of each plate and pour soup over it. (Serves 4 to 6.)

Too much salt in the soup? A raw potato, or part of one, added to it absorbs much of the excess salt.

SEAFOOD CHOWDER

This is a rich chowder which belongs in the meal-by-itself class. It makes a wonderful main course. For dinner, it should be followed by a hearty dessert. It may be frozen and reheated in the double boiler.

1 lb. fresh shrimps	3 cups milk
Salt and pepper	1 cup cream
1 onion, sliced	1 tsp. sherry OR a few drops of
1 carrot, sliced	Worcestershire sauce for each
1 stalk celery	serving
2 tbsp. butter	1 tsp. butter for each serving
2 small white onions, minced	Minced parsley
1 cup celery, finely chopped	

Wash shrimps, put them into a saucepan and cover with boiling water.

Add salt, pepper, onion, carrot and stalk of celery, and simmer until the shrimps turn pink and are tender (about 10 minutes).

Drain, and when shrimps are cool enough to handle, peel off the shells and clean them by removing the black line down the back.

Chop the shrimps very finely. (Two large cans of shrimps may be used if you prefer. They are less trouble but do not have the same fresh flavour.)

Melt butter in the top of a double boiler over direct heat.

Add onions, prepared shrimps and finely chopped celery. Cook slowly until the onions are softened and the shrimps well coated with butter (about 10 minutes).

Place the pan over boiling water and add milk. Season with salt and plenty of black pepper. When the soup is thoroughly heated again, add the cream and keep the chowder on the stove until it is piping hot.

Do not boil after milk and cream have been added.

Serve with a teaspoon of sherry or a few drops of Worcestershire sauce in each plate, plus a teaspoon of butter and a light sprinkling of parsley. (Serves 5.)

Note: Any shellfish such as lobster, chopped clams, finely flaked crab meat or a cup of flaked left-over fish may be used in place of shrimp.

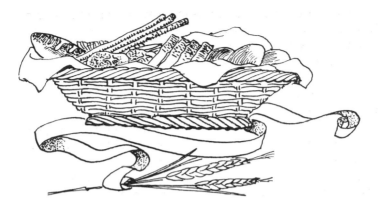

LILLIAN MOSHER'S FISH CHOWDER

I collected this recipe. sitting in Lillian Mosher's pretty ivy-papered kitchen near Lunenberg, N.S. Her bread was fresh out of the oven that evening, and I've never forgotten the smooth way she worked as she prepared the chowder. It was the first time I'd tasted the real thing made by a fisherman's wife.

1/8 lb. fat salt pork	1 1/2 lb. haddock fillets OR
2 large onions (finely chopped)	halibut
3 medium-sized potatoes (cut	1/2 cup boiling water
into small pieces)	1 large can evaporated milk
1 1/2 cups whole milk	(undiluted)

Sauté pork and remove scraps, allowing fat to remain in pot. Reserve scraps.

Add onions, potatoes, haddock fillets and boiling water. Simmer for 20 minutes.

Add evaporated milk, whole milk and the pork scraps previously removed. Season to taste. *Do not boil* after adding milk. (Serves 4 to 6.)

COLD BORSCHT

This is one of the versions I like best. I store it in the refrigerator for as long as two weeks in clean, tightly covered jars.

2 bunches beets
1 qt. water
Juice of 1 1/2 lemons
1/2 tsp. citric acid (sour salt)
   (bought at delicatessen or
   grocery store)

4 tbsp. sugar
2 tsp. salt
3/4 tsp. ground ginger
Chopped celery, chives, shallots
   OR cucumber
Sour cream

Cut off tops and ends of beets, scrub beets with a brush and cook in 1 quart water over medium heat. When beets are tender but not soft, remove from heat and allow to cool in their liquid.

Strain and keep the water in which beets were cooked; skin and grate beets finely.

Measure beets and add twice as much liquid (beet water and additional water). If too thick, add more water.

Heat to boiling, skim and add lemon juice, citric acid, sugar, salt and ginger. (Citric acid is a product made for Jewish cookery. It can be left out but I don't.) Add more seasonings, if desired.

Serve with chopped celery, chives, shallots or cucumber sprinkled on top and pass a bowl of sour cream. A hot, boiled potato placed in the cold soup is a delicious addition, or you can make potato balls with a melon cutter. (Makes 2 quarts.)

Canned consommé becomes a hearty soup when small balls of ground beef, combined with any favourite herbs and rolled in flour to keep them firm, are added and cooked for 15 minutes.

ALMOND AND TOMATO SOUP

This is one of our favourite summer soups. It's easy, does not have to be cooked and may be prepared well in advance of the meal. People who normally hold cold soups in disdain seem to like this one.

1 can condensed tomato soup	2 tbsp. parsley, chopped finely
1/2 cup condensed OR whole milk	Pinch of curry powder
3/4 cup table cream	Salt and pepper (to taste)
Few tablespoons celery, chopped	3 fresh limes OR lemons
finely	1 dozen blanched almonds

Combine soup, milk, cream, celery, parsley, curry, salt and pepper and chill in refrigerator for several hours.

When ready to serve, pour a tablespoon (or more or less) of lime or lemon juice in the bottom of each soup cup, and add a few slivered almonds.

Pour soup over almonds and lime or lemon juice and let each guest stir his own. If the soup appears too thick, add more cream or milk. (Serves 4 to 6.)

WATERCRESS SOUP

A cooling start to a meal on a hot night. The electric blender or food processor comes in handy here and with all soups which must be creamy and well combined.

1 bunch fresh watercress	1 tbsp. flour
2 tbsp. butter	1 qt. chicken stock
2 egg yolks	Salt and pepper

Wash watercress carefully and bring to a boil in cold water. Boil for 2 to 3 minutes.

Drain and chop finely.

Blend with butter, egg yolks and flour in electric blender or rub through strainer.

Place in a saucepan with chicken stock.

Simmer gently for 15 minutes. Season to taste and chill.

Serve in chilled bouillon cups sprinkled with sprigs of watercress. (Serves 6.)

BROCCOLI SOUP

Frozen peas or asparagus may be used in the same fashion as frozen broccoli is used in this recipe. I enjoy it best cold because its colour is so cool and it is more refreshing than hot soup. Increase the amount of chicken stock if you like. Do keep chicken cubes on hand for adding to soups.

3 tbsp. butter

1/4 cup onions, diced

1/4 cup celery, diced

1 lb. fresh broccoli OR

1 box frozen broccoli

1 cup milk

1 cup cream

1 tsp. salt

1/4 tsp. pepper

1/4 tsp. curry powder

1/2 cup chicken stock OR consommé

Melt butter, add onions and celery and cook, covered, for 5 minutes over low heat.

Add fresh, diced broccoli or frozen broccoli.

Add stock or consommé.

Cook till broccoli is tender.

Add remaining ingredients, and cook for 10 minutes longer. Do not boil.

Blend in electric blender or food processor or press through a sieve.

Chill and serve in chilled cups or plates . (Serves 4 to 5.)

Part 2

Middles

Stews, Casseroles, Meat Loaves

I favour the meat that allows for left-overs. Any cook whose time in the kitchen is limited appreciates those dishes which reheat well — stew, ragoût, daube, goulash. Pot roasts, too, are a great family dish but they are also the thing to serve to the person who lives alone or who is used to eating out in good restaurants — to them, pot roasts are a treat and very often a nostalgic reminder of childhood and home cooking. Hearty meat dishes, of course, are part of Canadian life — they get us through the winter.

HAM AND VEAL CASSEROLE

4-oz. egg noodles
1 lb. cooked ham cut into 1-inch
    pieces
1-lb. veal shoulder cut into 1-inch
    pieces
2/3 cup onions, minced

1/4 tsp. pepper
1/2 tsp. salt
1 tin beef gravy
Parsley (to decorate)
Ripe olives, sliced
Pinch of nutmeg

Cook noodles according to directions on package.

Trim some fat from the ham. Place fat in a frying pan and cook until partly melted.

Add onions, nutmeg, pepper and salt. Stir and cook over medium heat until onions are slightly brown.

Add ham and veal and stir over quick heat long enough to sear the meat. Remove fat.

Add beef gravy (if you like more sauce add 2 tins of beef gravy), scraping the bottom of the pan until all the ingredients are well blended. Taste for seasoning.

Cover pan and simmer 30 minutes or until meat is tender.

Line casserole with cooked noodles and pour in meat mixture. Top with parsley, olives. (Serves 4 to 6.)

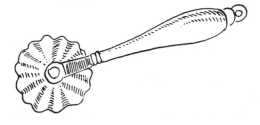

SWISS HAM QUICHE

1 uncooked pie shell
3/4 cup milk, scalded
1 tsp. minced chives OR green
    onions
1/4 tsp. salt

Dash nutmeg
2 eggs, slightly beaten
1/2 cup grated cheese
1 1/2 cups ground cooked ham
Dash pepper

Line a 9-inch pie plate with dough. Chill.

Add milk and seasoning to beaten eggs. Add cheese and ham.

Fill chilled crust.

Bake 15 minutes in a 450-degree oven.

Lower the heat to 350 degrees and bake 30 minutes longer. (Serves 4 to 5.)

LEFT-OVER HAM CASSEROLE

8 slices day-old bread	3 eggs, slightly beaten
1/4 cup butter	1 1/2 cups milk
2 cups ground cooked ham	1 8-oz. tin tomato sauce
2 tbsp. prepared mustard	1 tsp. salt
2 cups grated Cheddar cheese	Dash of pepper

Remove crusts from bread and spread with softened butter. Arrange 4 slices in a greased pan or casserole.

Mix ham with mustard and spread over bread.

Sprinkle about 1 1/4 cups of cheese over ham and cover with remaining slices of bread.

Combine eggs, milk, tomato sauce, salt and pepper.

Pour over bread and sprinkle with remaining cheese.

Chill for 1 hour to allow bread to absorb flavours.

Bake in a 325-degree oven till brown and serve at once. (Serves 4 to 6.)

HAM LOAF WITH HORSERADISH

3 lb. ground, uncooked smoked ham	1 1/2 cups buttermilk
2 eggs, slightly beaten	2 tbsp. brown sugar
3 cups fine, soft bread crumbs	2 tbsp. prepared horseradish
Salt to taste	Whipping cream

Combine all ingredients except cream.

Pack into greased loaf pan or an 8 x 8-inch baking pan or glass oven dish.

Bake in 350-degree oven for 1 1/2 hours, increasing the heat to 400 degrees for the last 15 minutes to brown a little.

Serve with whipped cream, mixed with a pinch of salt and additional horseradish (drained) to taste. (Serves 10 to 12.

PIGS' FEET

6 pigs' feet	2 onions, chopped
Salted water	1/4 cup wine vinegar OR 1/4 cup
2 bay leaves	apple juice
6 whole cloves	Salt and pepper
1 carrot, chopped	1 tbsp. corn syrup
1/2 cup chopped celery and leaves	2 to 3 tsp. cornstarch

Have butcher split the feet and cut into several pieces. Scrub them well.

Cover meat with cold, salted water, bring to a boil and simmer for 10 minutes. Drain and cover with fresh water.

Add bay leaves, cloves, vegetables, vinegar or apple juice, salt and pepper. Cover and simmer for 2 hours or till meat is tender.

Cool feet in liquor, drain off fat, strain broth, add syrup and thicken with cornstarch.

Serve with mashed potatoes and maître d'hôtel butter. (Serves 4 to 6.)

MAÎTRE D'HÔTEL BUTTER

4 tbsp. butter	1/2 tsp. mustard
Salt and pepper	1 tbsp. parsley, chopped
2 tsp. lemon juice	

Soften butter, blend in all ingredients and store in refrigerator till meal is ready. Make it in advance and freeze in a roll. Slice off as needed for steaks, meat patties and fish.

APPLE PORK TENDERLOIN

1 pork tenderloin	2 tbsp. butter
1 tbsp. flour	1 unpeeled apple, thickly sliced
1/2 tsp. salt	1 tbsp. sherry (optional)
1/4 tsp. paprika	1/2 cup cream OR whole milk
1/8 tsp. sage OR marjoram	

Roll pork tenderloin in flour seasoned with salt, paprika, sage or marjoram.

Brown meat over medium heat in melted butter until evenly browned on both sides.

When brown, top with slices of apple and add sherry and cream or milk.

Cover and simmer over low heat for 30 minutes.

FAVOURITE CHOPS EN CASSEROLE

I first made this one fall day when we watched the last leaves fall and the wind was beginning to bite. It filled the house with a marvellous aroma. I cook it any time the weather begins to be hard on our spirits.

6 thick pork chops	1/2 cup brown sugar
Oil	2 tbsp. cinnamon
Tarragon	2 tbsp. butter
Salt and pepper	Juice of 1 lemon
4 apples, unpeeled	1/4 cup water
4 medium onions	

Rub chops with oil, sprinkle with tarragon, salt and pepper and brown over a high heat.

Arrange a bed of chopped, cored apples and sliced onions in a deep casserole. Sprinkle with half the brown sugar and cinnamon, mixed.

Place chops on the bed and sprinkle with remainder of sugar and cinnamon. Dot with butter.

Pour lemon juice and water over chops, cover and bake at 325 degrees for an hour or more; uncover during last 10 minutes.

Slicing up apples for a meal? Fruit kept in the refrigerator does not discolour as quickly on cutting as does the fruit stored at room temperature.

BROWN STEW OF PORK

Pigs' feet are delicious in this stew and should be used by the cook who wants an interesting change.

2 to 3 lb. pigs' feet OR stewing
   pork
1 tsp. coarse salt
1/4 tsp. pepper
1/2 tsp. cinnamon

1/8 tsp. nutmeg
2 tbsp. fat
4 to 6 cups water
1 cup onions, sautéed
1/4 tsp. cloves

Cut meat into good-sized pieces. Scrub well.

Roll each piece in a mixture of salt, pepper, cinnamon, cloves and nutmeg.

Melt fat in a heavy pot, preferably an iron one, and brown meat well. (The secret of a good stew is in the browning.) Add onions, which have been sautéed in a separate pan, and water.

Cover and simmer until the meat is tender, about 2 hours. (Serves 4 to 6.)

AMERICAN BEEF POT ROAST

4-to-5-lb. beef pot roast, any cut
2 tsp. salt
1/4 tsp. pepper
1 clove garlic (optional)
2 to 3 tbsp. fat
3/4 cup water
1 can tomato soup

4 tbsp. ketchup
1 tbsp. Worcestershire sauce
3 small onions, diced
2 or 3 tbsp. brown sugar
1/2 tsp. dry mustard
3 tbsp. lemon juice

Rub roast with salt, pepper and garlic and brown in hot fat. Add water, tomato soup, ketchup, Worcestershire sauce, onions and garlic. Cover and cook over low heat for 1 1/2 hours.

Mix remaining ingredients and pour over meat. Cover and continue cooking for an hour or until meat is tender.

Skim and pour off fat from gravy, then thicken with 2 tbsp. flour made into a paste with water. (Serves 4 to 6.)

CHIPPED BEEF CASSEROLE

A mention of President Eisenhower's breakfast one day in 1958 gave us another good idea for a hearty morning main course. Chipped beef is good on toast or mixed with scrambled eggs. For an after-theatre or after-curling party, the following chipped beef casserole is ideal.

1 large green pepper, sliced	2 cups milk
1/2 cup celery, sliced	1 can kernel corn
1 onion, chopped	Salt and pepper
4 tbsp. butter OR salad oil	1 egg, beaten
6 oz. chipped beef	1/2 cup melted butter OR
4 tbsp. flour	margarine
	1 1/2 cups dried bread crumbs

Sauté over low heat pepper, celery and onion in butter or oil till tender.

Place beef in a bowl of hot water, leave for 20 minutes, then drain.

Add beef to sautéed vegetables and stir in flour. Add milk slowly, stirring constantly.

Add corn, salt and pepper and beaten egg, and cook for a minute.

Brown melted butter or margarine and crumbs in a small pan and add to chipped beef.

Pour into a buttered casserole and bake at 325 degrees for 35 minutes. (Serves 8 to 10.)

UPSIDE-DOWN BEEF PIE

This is another answer to the request for recipes which can be prepared in a great hurry. It makes interesting use of ground beef, the most popular meat in Canada, according to the butchers.

2 onions, minced	2 tbsp. ketchup OR tomato paste
1 green pepper	1 tbsp. salt
2 tbsp. dripping OR butter	1/4 tsp. pepper
1 lb. ground beef	1/4 tsp. savory
1 8-oz. can tomato sauce	1/2 tsp. dry mustard

Sauté onion and green pepper in fat or butter, add beef and stir until the red colour disappears.

Add remaining ingredients and cook together for a few minutes.

Turn into a shallow pudding dish and cover with the topping (recipe follows) or with a packaged biscuit mix.

Bake in a 400-degree oven for 25 minutes.

To serve, turn upside down on hot service plate.

TOPPING

2 cups all-purpose flour, sifted	1/3 cup salad oil OR melted
3 tsp. baking powder	shortening
1 tsp. salt	2/3 cup milk

Sift flour, baking powder and salt together.

Quickly stir in oil or melted shortening mixed with the milk.

Turn dough on floured board and roll out to fit casserole. Place on top, brush with milk and bake. (Serves 6.)

RICH OXTAIL STEW

2 oxtails (about 3 lb.)	1/2 tsp. monosodium glutamate
2 tbsp. shortening OR salad oil	2 medium onions, chopped
2 cups water	2 1/2 cups tomatoes
1 tbsp. salt	1 tbsp. sugar
1/4 tsp. pepper	Chopped parsley

Have butcher cut oxtails into medium pieces or do it yourself.

Heat shortening or salad oil in a heavy pan, add oxtails and brown well on all sides.

Add water, seasonings and onions, cover tightly and cook over low heat for about 2 hours.

Add tomatoes and sugar and continue cooking till meat is easily pierced with a fork.

Serve stew sprinkled with chopped parsley. Hot, buttered noodles, sprinkled with poppy seeds, are a delicious accompaniment. (Serves 4 to 6.)

STEAK AND KIDNEY PIE

1 cup beef suet
1 beef kidney
1 lb. round beefsteak
1/2 cup browned flour
3 medium onions, sliced
3 cups hot water

1 tsp. salt
1/2 tsp. pepper
1 tsp. mustard
1 cup cold water
Pastry

Melt suet in a cast-iron pot or a skillet.

Dice kidney and steak while fat is melting, and roll in browned flour. Set aside remaining flour.

Place floured meat in hot fat and turn over quick heat until meat is seared.

Add onions and stir until well blended.

Add hot water, salt, pepper and mustard. Bring to a boil, stirring all the time.

Cover and simmer over low heat until kidney and steak are tender.

Thicken to taste with the remainder of browned flour mixed with 1 cup of cold water.

Place in a casserole, cover with your favourite pastry, in which a few small slits have been made.

Bake at 400 degrees till well browned. (Serves 4.)

FAMILY MEAT LOAF

2 1/2 lb. ground round steak
2 to 4 tbsp. horseradish
3 tbsp. ketchup
1 tsp. salt
1/2 tsp. pepper

1/2 cup whole milk OR light cream
6 slices bacon
2 medium onions
1 1/4 cups crushed crackers
1/2 cup water OR stock

Combine steak, horseradish, ketchup, salt, pepper and milk or cream.

Grind bacon, onions and 1 cup of crackers in meat chopper or blender and add to meat mixture.

Use hands to knead the mixture and mould into loaf shape.

Roll loaf in remaining 1/4 cup of crackers.

Place loaf in a shallow baking pan.

Pour water or stock into the same pan and bake at 350 degrees for 1 1/2 hours. During baking, baste occasionally and add more liquid if necessary.

Serve hot with drippings which have been thickened with flour. (Serves 8.)

SURPRISE MEATBALLS

Dried fruit add nutrition to the winter diet and can be used to surprise children in this way. Apricots and pears are wonderful when added to a dish of cabbage rolls — they stretch the budget.

12 cooked prunes	1 1/2 tsp. salt
1 slice canned pineapple	Dash of pepper
1 egg	Cooking oil
1 1/2 lb. ground lean beef	1/2 cup mushrooms
1/2 cup fine dry bread crumbs	1 cup water
1/2 cup milk	1 tbsp. flour

Pit prunes and stuff each with a small wedge of pineapple.

Beat egg lightly and blend with beef, crumbs, milk, salt and pepper.

Shape beef mixture into balls around stuffed prunes, covering each prune completely. Brown on all sides in a little hot oil.

Add mushrooms and water, cover and cook slowly 20 to 30 minutes. Thicken sauce. (Serves 6.)

Hamburger will be juicier and more tender if you add a quarter of a cup of water to each pound of meat before cooking.

PRACTICAL MEAT LOAF

This isn't a basic cookbook but basic recipes for meat loaves are bound to find their way into the collection of anyone who cooks every day.

1 onion, chopped
1 green pepper OR pimiento
1/8 tsp. celery salt
Dash nutmeg
1 clove garlic, minced
1/4 cup chopped celery and leaves
1 lb. ground beef OR left-over
   ham, goose or duck
1 egg
1/2 cup Parmesan cheese, grated

1/2 cup wheat germ OR bread
   crumbs
1/3 cup powdered milk
3 tbsp. ground parsley
1/2 tsp. black pepper
3 tsp. salt
1/2 cup fresh milk
Pinch thyme
Pinch of basil
Paprika

Sauté lightly onion, green pepper or pimiento, celery salt, nutmeg and garlic in a small amount of butter or salad oil. Remove from heat and add remainder of ingredients. Mix thoroughly, preferably with fingers.

Pack into an oiled loaf pan or ring mould.

Sprinkle generously with paprika.

Bake in a moderate oven (350 degrees) for about 40 minutes.

Serve hot or cold.   If ring mould is used fill centre of meat loaf with black and stuffed olives and carrot sticks. (Serves 6.)

CORNED BEEF AND CABBAGE

A hearty Canadian dish

4-to-5-lb. brisket of corned beef
1/2 lb. salt pork (optional)
8 carrots, scraped
6 to 8 parsnips, peeled

8 onions peeled
Potatoes (to taste)
1 medium-sized head of cabbage,
   cored and quartered

Place corned beef in a large kettle. Cover with cold water and simmer, covered, for 2 hours.

Add salt pork (optional) and simmer another 2 hours.

Skim carefully to remove excess fat. Add carrots, parsnips and onions, and cover and cook for 30 minutes.

Add potatoes to taste (I usually boil 10 to 14 potatoes, reserving 6 to 8 to make corned-beef hash the next day), and continue cooking until potatoes are tender. Cabbage should be added about 10 to 15 minutes before serving.

Place meat in centre of a big platter, surround with vegetables and garnish with parsley. (Serves 4 to 5.)

HOT SAUCES FOR CORNED BEEF OR HAM

HOT MUSTARD SAUCE

1/2 cup cider vinegar	1 tbsp. sugar
1 tbsp. butter	2 tbsp. prepared mustard
1 egg, beaten	1 tbsp. paprika

Combine ingredients in a saucepan. Stir and cook over low heat until thickened. Pour over corned beef when ready to serve.

EASY MUSTARD SAUCE

1 tbsp. butter OR margarine	1/2 tsp. salt
1 tbsp. flour	2 tbsp. prepared mustard
1 cup milk	

Melt butter or margarine in a saucepan. Blend in flour, mixing well. Add milk slowly, stirring constantly until mixture boils and thickens. Cook 3 to 5 minutes longer until starch is thoroughly cooked. Add salt and prepared mustard.

Flour will not mess up cupboard shelves and other utensils if sifter is kept on a base. Rubber or china flowerpot holder is ideal.

ONION SAUCE

2 onions, sliced	1 cup beef bouillon
2 tbsp. sugar	1 tsp. vinegar
1 tbsp. fat	1 tsp. paprika
1 tbsp. flour	

Cook onions and sugar together in fat until onions are lightly browned. Stir in flour, beef bouillon, vinegar and paprika. Stir and cook until smooth and thick.

GLAZED CORNED BEEF À L'ANGLAISE

5 lb. corned beef (brisket or bottom round)	1 onion, cut in 4
2 quarts hot water	Whole cloves
2 stalks celery with leaves	1/4 cup brown sugar
1 tbsp. brown sugar	1 1/2 tsp. dry mustard
	4 tbsp. apple juice

Place corned beef in saucepan and cover with water.

Add celery, 1 tbsp. brown sugar and onion. Bring to a boil, lower heat, cover and simmer for 4 hours or until beef is tender.

Remove meat from broth and place in a shallow pan with fat side up. Score fat diagonally to form diamonds. Stud each square with whole cloves. Mix 1/4 cup brown sugar, dry mustard and apple juice together and spread on top of meat.

Bake in a 400-degree oven for 15 to 25 minutes until well glazed. Baste 3 or 4 times during cooking period and after meat is removed from oven, with the juice that has accumulated in the pan. (Serves 4 to 6.)

Note: This is very good served with new potatoes or baked potatoes and a casserole of onions. It can be cooked in the morning or even a day ahead. If you wish to serve it hot, reheat in the broth and glaze just before serving.

BOILED BEEF

I like this as well as corned beef, and it is an answer to the needs of anyone who goes out to work and wants to prepare dishes in advance. This can be cooked one night and, depending on the size of the piece of beef, stretched over two dinners, since it takes beautifully to reheating.

5 lb. rump bottom round, brisket or short ribs of beef	1 onion
	1 carrot
2 1/2 tsp. salt	Sprig of parsley
1 bay leaf	

Place meat in a deep kettle and add remaining ingredients.
Add enough hot water to cover half the meat, cover and simmer (never boil) till tender. This will take from 3 to 4 hours. The meat should be tender enough to cut easily into slices without being stringy or soggy. During the last hour of cooking, whole carrots and onions can be added to the kettle and they take on all the flavours in the pot.

To serve cold, beef should be left to cool in its broth. Store meat in a bowl or plate with a little of the broth, and place a plate on top, weighing it down with a heavy stone or iron. A soup plate is ideal since it will press down on the meat. Pressure helps give shape to the meat, making slicing easier. Boiled beef is delicious eaten with horseradish. (Serves 5 to 6.)

GINGER BEEF PIE

3 lb. economy cut beef	1 tsp. black pepper
Meat tenderizer (optional)	1/4 tsp. dried tarragon
2 tbsp. margarine OR suet	1/4 tsp. ground ginger
1 cup consommé	1/4 tsp. ground cinnamon
6 small onions, skinned and chopped	3/4 cup red wine OR 1/2 cup consommé OR water
4 small carrots, diced	Pastry for 1-crust pie
1/4 lb. sliced mushrooms OR button mushrooms	Butter OR margarine

Tenderize meat if desired according to directions on package or bottle.

Wipe meat with clean, damp cloth. Cube.

Sauté in margarine or suet till light brown, then cook slowly with consommé for 1 hour.

Add onions, carrots, mushrooms, seasonings. Cook slowly for 30 minutes.

Pour into baking dish. Add wine, consommé or water; top with pastry; crimp rim; slash top decoratively to let the steam out. Brush top with butter or margarine.

Bake in a 425-degree oven for 20 to 30 minutes. (Serves 8.)

HERBED SWISS STEAK

Recipes for Swiss Steak are a dime a dozen, but I wanted to include this one because it is so good and I know readers who like simple recipes will appreciate it.

3 lb. top round steak (2 inches thick)	1 tsp. marjoram
2/3 cup flour	1/2 tsp. summer savory
1/2 tsp. salt	1 clove garlic
1/8 tsp. pepper	1 onion
Suet OR fat	1/2 cup dry white wine (optional)
Cayenne pepper	1/4 cup boiling water

Pound flour, salt and pepper into meat. This takes time and you will have to leave the meat for half an hour at a time to allow it to absorb the flour.

Melt suet or fat in a Dutch oven or frying pan with cover.

Brown the steak, sprinkle it with cayenne, marjoram, savory and minced garlic. Slice the onion and lay the slices on the meat.

Pour wine and water (if wine is not used, simply use a little more water) gently around the meat so that seasonings are left on the meat.

Cover the pan and simmer for 2 hours, basting with the liquid in the pan.

Add salt during the last half hour if it is needed.

Serve on a large platter with the gravy. (Serves 6.)

FRENCH POT ROAST

A very good dish which gets better with re-heating. The gravy is superb because it is made of meat juices and the vegetables which have cooked in them. No flour is added for thickening.

4-to-5-lb. rump or round roast	1 tsp. salt
1/4 cup beef suet, minced	1/2 tsp. pepper
1/2 cup carrots, diced	1 bay leaf
3 onions, sliced	1/4 tsp. thyme
2 sticks celery, diced	1 tsp. dry mustard
1 clove garlic, finely chopped	1/2 cup red wine OR consommé

Place suet in a heavy cast-iron kettle and melt. Add prepared vegetables and cook over steady heat, stirring frequently, until vegetables are lightly browned.

Remove vegetables from kettle, leaving as much fat as possible. Slip garlic in under fat part of meat and brown meat on all sides, turning it with two wooden spoons. Do not pierce it with a fork. Season with salt and pepper; add bay leaf, thyme and mustard. Spoon vegetables over meat and stir together. Add wine or consommé.

Cover kettle and place over moderate heat or in a 350-degree oven for 1 1/2 to 2 hours or until meat is tender.

To serve, lift the roast from the kettle and place on a hot platter. Strain the gravy through a sieve or blender. (Serves 6.)

SWEET-SOUR POT ROAST

Sweet and sour is usually associated with oriental dishes, but here is a western idea which combines the contradictory tastes.

5 lb. pot roast	1 tbsp. salt
2 tbsp. fat	Pepper (to taste)
1 carrot	1/4 cup vinegar
1/2 cup celery, chopped	1/2 cup light or dark raisins
1 onion, sliced	1 tbsp. cornstarch

Wipe meat with a damp cloth and brown on all sides in hot fat.

Scrape carrot, cut into small pieces, and add with celery and onion to meat. Add seasonings, vinegar and raisins. Cover and cook until tender (1 1/2 to 2 hours), adding a little water.

Remove meat to platter and keep hot while thickening drippings for gravy. Stir cornstarch into a little cold water, then into drippings. (Serves 6 to 8.)

BROWN BEEF STEW

2 lb. chuck beef, cut into 1 1/2-inch cubes	1 tbsp. salt
2 tbsp. fat	1/2 tsp. pepper
4 cups boiling water	1/2 tsp. paprika
1 tsp. lemon juice	Dash allspice OR cloves
1 tsp. Worcestershire sauce	1 tsp. sugar
1 clove garlic	6 carrots, cut into quarters
1 medium-sized onion, sliced	1 lb. small white onions
2 bay leaves	2 tbsp. flour
	1/4 cup cold water

Brown meat thoroughly on all sides in hot fat.

Add water, lemon juice, Worcestershire sauce, garlic, onion, bay leaves, salt, pepper, paprika, allspice or cloves and sugar. Simmer for 2 hours, stirring occasionally to keep from sticking.

Add carrots and onions and continue cooking for 20 to 30 minutes or until vegetables are done.

Thicken liquid with flour blended with cold water to make gravy.

Cook 10 minutes longer. Cubed potatoes may be added if desired. (Serves 6 to 8.)

SHEPHERD'S PIE

The Empress Hotel in Victoria, B.C. serves the best Shepherd's Pie I've ever eaten. They make it with left-over beef.

2 cups chopped cooked beef	1/4 cup parsley, chopped
1 onion, chopped	1-2 cups gravy
1 clove garlic, chopped	Mashed potatoes
4 tbsp. butter	2 egg yolks
Salt and pepper	3 tbsp. butter

Chop cooked beef but do not grind it.

Cook chopped onion in 4 tbsp. butter till golden and soft, add chopped garlic, beef, salt and pepper to taste, parsley, then gravy. Stir till all is warm.

Pour into greased casserole and top with freshly-mashed potatoes to which you've added two egg yolks and salt and pepper, to taste. Use a pastry bag with a meringue tube to pipe the potatoes on top of the pie for a very appetizing effect. Never add milk or cream to potatoes when you plan to pipe them through a pastry bag. Dot with bits of butter and place in 375 degree oven for 25-30 minutes.   Serves 4.

GLAZE FOR BUFFET DISHES

Professional chefs fill the home cook with envy when they prepare a display of glazed meats and pâtés. But you can do it at home the following way.

1 envelope unflavoured gelatin   1 tin consommé
1/4 cup cold water

Add gelatin to cold water and leave for 5 minutes.

Heat consommé and add gelatin and stir over heat until dissolved (about 4 minutes).

Place in refrigerator until liquid begins to jell — about the consistency of egg-whites. With a spatula or brush spread mixture over food to be glazed and place in refrigerator.

Glaze may not spread evenly at first, but after 1 hour in the refrigerator it can be spread to satisfaction. (Glazed food should be kept cool at all times.)

BLENDER MUSTARD

1/4 lb. dry mustard
1/4 tsp. pepper
1/2 cup brown sugar
1/2 cup lemon juice, fresh, canned
   or frozen OR vinegar

1/2 cup salad OR olive oil
1/4 to 1/2 cup coarse salt, Tabasco
   OR horseradish OR 1/2 tsp.
   marjoram, basil OR tarragon for
   a spicy flavour

Place all ingredients in blender, cover and blend fast for 1/2 minute.

Store in sterilized jar and allow to stand one week. This mustard will keep in the cupboard for six months and doesn't have to be stored in the refrigerator.

SAUERKRAUT SUPPER

2 large cans sauerkraut
6 wieners
6 slices bacon OR cooked ham
6 slices of salami OR
   any spiced meat

1 Polish OR other large European
   sausage
Apple juice, white wine, beer
   OR water (optional)

Place sauerkraut in bottom of oven dish or in electric frying pan.

Arrange wieners (skins removed), bacon or ham, salami or other spiced meat and unsliced sausage on top.

Cover and cook over medium heat or in medium oven for half an hour or more. Longer cooking doesn't do any harm. If desired, apple juice, wine, beer or water may be added to sauerkraut for extra flavour and also to provide more juice.

Serve with mustard and pumpernickel, rye or other dark bread and follow with a light dessert. (Serves 4-6.)

JELLIED VEAL LOAF

6 lb. veal knuckle
2 onions, sliced
1 bunch celery tops
1 clove garlic
1/2 tsp. pepper
2 bay leaves
1/4 tsp. thyme
Pinch of sage
2 cloves
Handful of parsley

2 tbsp. salt
3 tbsp. lemon juice
4 cups fresh peas, drained and cooked
5 or 6 hard-cooked eggs, sliced
Stuffed olives, sliced
1 tin shrimp, drained and cleaned
   (if desired)
2 envelopes plain gelatin
1/4 cup cold water

Place in a large kettle veal knuckle, onions, celery tops, garlic, pepper, bay leaves, thyme, sage, cloves, parsley and salt.

Simmer from 3 to 4 hours until meat is tender.

Remove meat, strain the stock and let it cool. When cool, taste to see if it requires more salt.

Skim off all the fat. Add lemon juice and if stock measures more than 1 quart, boil rapidly until it is down to the right amount.

Meanwhile take the meat from the veal bones and cut it into small cubes. Mix together with peas.

Decorate the bottom of a very large mould (or use two 8-or-9-inch ring moulds or plain round moulds) with sliced eggs and as many sliced, stuffed olives as you require. One tin of drained, cleaned shrimps will also give a touch of colour.

Soak gelatin in cold water for 5 minutes. Add hot veal stock and stir until gelatin is dissolved.

Place the meat and peas carefully in the moulds so as not to displace your design. Pour the hot veal stock over slowly.

Cool and place in the refrigerator for at least 6 hours or overnight. (Serves 6.)

Meat

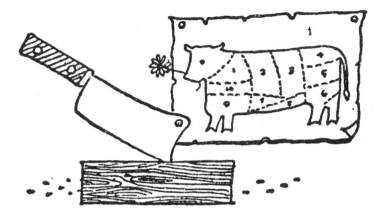

In spite of increased food costs, I still prefer to buy a large roast — it has more flavour and more juice, and I find I get more for my money in the long run.   An 8-lb. roast of beef, for example, will give our household at least three meals, plus thin   strips for marinated salad and at least one delectable Shepherd's Pie — my preferred left-over dish. The food processor called Cuisinart (Magi-Mix in France) described in the chapter on utensils is fantastic with leftovers — you turn out delectable spreads with cooked meats and they make excellent lunch box sandwiches as well as appetizers.

The clay pot deserves a mention here. It is the busy cook's best friend. It allows you or anyone who happens to be at home in the late afternoon to put meat into the oven without first browning it and there's no tending, no basting, no watching required. Children can prepare a main course in the clay pot with minimum instructions. It's a good trick to brush meat or chicken all over with soy sauce before roasting — extra flavour is added as well as an appetizing browned appearance.

OVEN-BROILED STEAK

Cheap cuts of beef should never be placed under the broiler which was designed for tender morsels.

Club, T-bone, Spencer, rib, sirloin
   or filet mignon steaks cut
   approximately 1 inch thick

Olive OR salad oil
Paprika
Garlic OR garlic salt (optional)

Remove steak from refrigerator half an hour before cooking to allow it to come to room temperature. Rub with garlic. Brush meat with a light coating of olive or salad oil, and sprinkle generously with paprika and garlic salt.

Place on broiler rack of oven and set 2 inches away from heat. Leave oven door slightly open.

Cook 10 minutes on one side and 5 minutes on the other if you wish to have your steak medium done. When using low heat, cook 20 minutes on one side and 5 minutes on the other.

(For a less tender cut of steak, 1 inch thick, always cook it in a pan over a low flame for 25 minutes on one side and 10 minutes on the other).

PERFECT ROAST BEEF

1 roast of beef
3 tbsp. fat
1 tbsp. dry mustard

Garlic (to taste)
1 tbsp. salt for 4 to 5 lb. of meat

Combine fat (any kind), mustard (never the prepared variety) and garlic. (Increase amounts for very large roast.)

Spread this paste on the raw meat. This keeps the natural juices inside and prevents the roast from drying out.

Sprinkle with salt.

Place on rack in pan and bake uncovered at 350 degrees 18 minutes per pound for medium rare. Reduce cooking time if very rare meat is desired. Do not baste.

MINCED BEEF MIGNON

2 lb. lean raw ground beef
1/4 cup evaporated milk
Salt and pepper (to taste)
1/4 tsp. cloves
1/4 tsp. sage

1/4 tsp. nutmeg
2 tbsp. onion, grated
2 tbsp. parsley, chopped
1 tsp. Worcestershire sauce
6 bacon slices

Mix together all ingredients except bacon. Form into 6 thick patties of equal size.

Wrap each patty in a bacon slice and skewer with a toothpick.

Cook patties in a hot frying pan, rolling to make sure bacon is thoroughly done.

Brown 5 minutes on each side.

Place on freshly made toast rounds.

Garnish each platter with watercress or parsley, and pour over each patty 1 generous tablespoon of brown sauce made by adding 1/2 cup water and 1 tsp. meat extract to a little of the fat left in the pan. (Serves 6.)

SPARERIBS AND SAUERKRAUT

Bacon
2 lb. or 2 cans sauerkraut
3 to 4 Spanish onions, sliced

2 lb. spareribs
Salt, pepper and paprika

Line a casserole or baking pan with bacon strips.

Arrange sauerkraut on the bacon, heaping it up in the middle.

Arrange onion slices on sauerkraut and over this arrange spareribs which have been seasoned with salt, pepper and paprika.

Roast in a 350-degree oven for 1 1/2 hours (or more) till spareribs are beautifully brown and thoroughly cooked.

Eat with apple sauce to which horseradish has been added, and buttered squash which has been baked with the spareribs. (Serves 4.)

DANISH SPARERIBS

4 lb. spareribs
1 cup water
1 lb. prunes, pitted

6 apples
1 tsp. salt
1/2 tsp. pepper

Have butcher crack ribs along the middle. Leave ribs in rack form.

Pour water over prunes and bring to the boil.

Remove from heat and allow to soak for 5 minutes.

Peel apples, remove cores and cut into 1/4-inch slices. Add to prunes.

Drain prunes and apples. Arrange ribs, seasoned with salt and pepper, on a shallow roasting pan. Cover with half of the apple-and-prune mixture and fold over where ribs have been cracked. Secure with skewers.

Roast in a 350-degree oven for 1 1/2 hours or more. If pan dries out during baking, add a little hot water several times.

Serve with a sauce made from pan drippings, adding a few tablespoons of apple jelly. (Serves 8.)

TANGY BARBECUED RIBS

3 to 4 lb. spareribs
1/3 cup fresh lemon juice
1/3 cup ketchup OR chili sauce
1 tsp. horseradish sauce
1 tsp. salt
Dash of Tabasco
1 tbsp. Worcestershire sauce

1/2 cup fresh orange juice
2 tsp. dry mustard
1/2 tsp. paprika
1/4 cup honey OR brown sugar
1 garlic clove
2 lemons, unpeeled and sliced

Cut ribs into pieces, place in a roasting pan and brown at 450 degrees for 45 to 50 minutes. Drain off fat.

Combine remaining ingredients with exception of lemon slices and brush over ribs.

Place lemon slices over meat and reduce heat to 350 degrees, and bake for 1 hour, basting frequently. (Serves 6.)

BAKED SPARERIBS AND SAUERKRAUT

3 to 4 lb. spareribs
1 large can sauerkraut

Salt and pepper
1/2 cup hot water

Place spareribs in roasting pan and bake, uncovered, in a 400-degree oven for 30 minutes. Remove ribs. If there is a lot of fat, pour off most of it.

Put sauerkraut in roasting pan, arrange spareribs on top, season with salt and pepper, add hot water, cover and bake at 350 degrees for 1 hour. (Serves 6.)

ROAST LAMB WITH ROSEMARY

Rosemary and lamb were made for each other. Herbs should be replaced frequently for they lose their fragrance and potency easily. Buy them in small bottles or grow your own.

4-to-5-lb. leg or loin of lamb
1/2 lemon
Salt and pepper (to taste)
1/4 tsp. crushed rosemary
1/2 cup salad oil

1 tbsp. dried mustard
1 tin condensed consommé
1 tbsp. brandy (optional)
1 small pinch rosemary

Rub leg or loin of lamb with lemon.

Sprinkle generously with salt, pepper and crushed rosemary.

Mix salad oil with dried mustard and brush it on top of roast.

Roast in a 350-degree oven for 20 to 25 minutes per pound. Pour off most of fat and discard.

Add to the roast drippings in the pan condensed consommé, brandy and rosemary. Do not add any thickening. This makes a delicious sauce.

Serve with broccoli and rice with parsley, and fresh pineapple-and-orange salad as a dessert.

SWEDISH GLAZED LAMB

1 4-to-5-lb. leg of lamb
Garlic
1 tbsp. salt
1 tsp. dry mustard

1 cup strong left-over coffee
  (or use instant coffee)
3 tbsp. currant jelly
2 tsp. cream

2 tbsp. brandy (optional)

Make gashes in lamb and stuff with small slivers of garlic.   Rub meat with salt and dry mustard.

Roast in a 350-degree oven for 25 minutes per pound.

Baste every 20 minutes with coffee mixed with jelly, cream and brandy.

GRAVY

3 tbsp. flour   3/4 cup cream   2 tbsp. currant jelly

Add flour to 3 tbsp. fat in pan.

Add cream slowly, stirring constantly.

Add jelly and stir till dissolved.

LAMB STEW WITH BISCUITS

5 lb. lamb shoulder, cut into
  small pieces
Salt and pepper
Flour
1/4 cup shortening OR salad oil
4 cups water
1/4 tsp. pepper
2 tsp. salt
1 clove garlic, minced

Pinch of marjoram
Pinch of thyme
1 tsp. dried dill OR crushed dill
  seeds
2 cups stock OR water
12 to 16 small carrots
1 lb. small white onions
1 pkg. frozen peas
Baking-powder biscuits

Place a little salt, pepper and flour in a paper bag and shake meat around until pieces are well coated.

Brown lamb on all sides in hot fat in a heavy kettle or frying pan.

Add 4 cups water, pepper, salt, garlic, herbs and cover tightly and simmer for 1 1/2 to 2 hours over low heat till meat is tender.

Remove meat and discard bones. Allow liquid to cool and skim off all fat. This stew is better done a day ahead of eating so that all fat may show itself and be removed.

Add 2 cups stock or water (or a bouillon cube diluted in water) to liquid remaining in stew pot, heat and scrape up any brown pieces stuck to the bottom of kettle. Cook carrots and onions in liquid, but cook peas separately. Thicken with a little additional flour if desired, taste for seasoning, add meat and peas and heat again.

Arrange vegetables attractively around stew in a shallow platter and decorate with hot biscuits (a mix is convenient) or serve biscuits in a basket. (Serves 8.)

ROAST PORK

Loin or leg of pork	1/2 tsp. marjoram
1/2 cup coarse salt	1 tsp. salt
Few cloves of garlic	1/4 tsp. pepper
1 tsp. dry mustard	1/4 tsp. monosodium glutamate (MSG)

Prepare pork, before roasting, as follows:

Place meat in an earthenware or glass dish and sprinkle with coarse salt. (Do not use fine salt.)

Cover dish and let stand 1 hour at room temperature.

Rinse under running water, dry and place in dripping pan.

Stuff roast to taste with garlic.

Rub top of meat with dry mustard and marjoram. Sprinkle with salt, pepper and monosodium glutamate.

Place 1/2 cup of water in roasting pan. Do not cover meat. Roast in a 325-degree oven, 50 minutes per pound.

(Roast pork, to be perfect, must cook in a slow oven for a long period of time. It does not require any basting. The gravy should always be made with flour, as it is too rich for a plain gravy.)

Carrots should be cut on the length rather than crosswise. Nutritionists say that food value is lost when vegetable is cut and cooked in round shapes.

117

ROAST PORK WITH ANISE

1 pork roast
Salt and pepper
1 tbsp. parsley, minced
1 garlic clove, minced
Flour

1 cup chicken stock
1/2 cup white wine OR apple juice
1 tbsp. anise seed OR
1 tbsp. dried dill

Sprinkle roast with salt and pepper and make several deep slits with a sharp knife.

Fill gashes with combined parsley and garlic.

Rub roast with flour and place in a 350-degree oven for 30 minutes.

Combine stock (or 2 chicken bouillon cubes in one cup of boiling water), wine and anise seed (which can be bought at most grocery stores) or dill and simmer 15 minutes.

Reduce heat to 300 degrees at the end of the first half-hour and roast until pork is well done (allow 40 minutes per pound). Every 15 minutes, pour on some of the stock mixture and when it is finished baste with pan gravy.

Serve pork with gravy from pan.

HAM IN SPIRITS

1 ham, 4 to 6 lb.
1 1/2 cups brown sugar
1 1/2 cups red or white wine, beer,
    ginger ale, cider OR apple juice

1 lemon, rind and juice
1 cup of water
1 tbsp. ground cloves
1 cup raisins, cherries OR pineapple

Soak ham overnight, unless it is partially cooked.

Place in a covered roaster or clay baker.

Mix all ingredients except fruit and pour over ham.

Cover tightly and roast at 325 degrees 30 minutes per lb. (If ham is partially cooked, reduce cooking to 15 minutes per lb.)

Uncover roaster, carefully remove rind, and leave fat as is.

Baste well with liquid in pan, add fruit, cover and roast till very tender.

Before serving, thicken the sauce with a teaspoon of cornstarch blended in a little cold water.

If you like, you may glaze the ham by patting the ham all over with brown sugar and placing in a 400-degree oven, uncovered, till golden brown.   (Serves 8 to 10.)

VERA CRUZ HAM SLICE

This is a good Easter dinner dish for the household which doesn't like left-over ham.   It's ideal for the apartment dwellers or for the single person living alone.   The sauce may be made in advance and frozen.

1 ham steak, large and thick
1/4 cup butter
3 tbsp. flour
1 1/2 cups consommé
2/3 cup seedless raisins

1/2 cup almonds, blanched and
    slivered
1/2 cup sherry OR orange juice
6 very thin slices lemon, unpeeled,
    and cut in halves
1/4 tsp. ground cloves

Brown butter and stir in flour.

Add consommé, raisins, almonds, sherry or orange juice, lemon and ground cloves.

Boil gently until well blended and pour over lightly buttered ham steak.

Cover and bake in a 325-degree oven for 1 hour.   (Allow 1/2 lb. for each person.)

SAUCES TO SERVE WITH HAM

CURRANT-HORSERADISH SAUCE

1/3 cup prepared horseradish   1 glass (6 oz.) currant jelly

Mix horseradish and jelly over low heat until thoroughly blended.

MUSTARD SAUCE

1 cup whole milk	1/4 tsp. salt
1/4 cup sugar	1 egg yolk, beaten
2 tbsp. dry mustard	1/4 cup hot cider OR apple juice
1 tbsp. all-purpose flour	

Heat 3/4 cup milk over low heat.

Mix sugar, mustard, flour and salt together and blend with remaining 1/4 cup milk.

Pour over beaten egg yolk and add to heated milk.

Stir and cook until thickened. Remove from heat and stir in cider or apple juice.

RAISIN SAUCE

2 tbsp. ham dripping	1 cup pineapple juice OR cider
2 tbsp. all-purpose flour	1/2 cup seedless raisins
1/2 tsp. dry mustard	1/4 cup sherry (optional)

Blend dripping, flour and mustard. Slowly add pineapple juice or cider.

Bring to boil, add raisins and simmer for 10 minutes.

Add sherry just before serving.

To make a smooth gravy, combine flour and water in jar, shake well and add to hot fat.

LAMB KIDNEYS AND MUSHROOMS

12 lamb kidneys
1 tbsp. lemon juice
3 tbsp. flour
1 1/2 cups celery, minced
1/3 cup onions, minced
6 tbsp. butter OR margarine

1 bouillon cube
1 cup boiling water
3/4 lb. mushrooms, washed and
   sliced
1/8 tsp. paprika
3 tbsp. sherry (optional)

Prepare kidneys and cut into quarters.

Sprinkle with lemon juice and dredge with flour.

Sauté celery and onion in butter or margarine until just tender. Remove and sauté kidneys in the butter until lightly browned.

Dissolve bouillon cube in boiling water. Add to kidneys with celery-onion mixture, mushrooms, paprika and salt.

Simmer, covered, for 25 minutes, stirring frequently. Add sherry.

Serve on fluffy rice, toast or mashed potatoes.
(Serves 6.)

BARBECUED BEEF LIVER

1 lb. beef liver cut in 1/4-inch
   slices (about 4)
Salt and pepper
1 cup onions, sliced and peeled
2 tbsp. butter OR margarine
1 tbsp. vinegar
1 tbsp. Worcestershire sauce

1 tsp. sugar
1/8 tsp. pepper
1 tsp. prepared mustard
1/8 tsp. chili powder
1/4 cup ketchup
1 tbsp. water

Cut liver slices in half crosswise.

Arrange half of them side by side, in a covered shallow baking dish (or arrange in a 9-inch pie plate and use another one for a cover).

Sprinkle lightly with salt and pepper.

Sauté onions in butter or margarine in skillet until lightly browned; arrange half on liver slices.

Combine vinegar with Worcestershire sauce, sugar, pepper, prepared mustard, chili powder, ketchup and water, then spoon 1 tsp. of this sauce over each pile of onions.

Arrange rest of liver slices on top of onions, then top with onions.

Cover dish and bake in a 325-degree oven for 25 minutes.

Uncover, spoon rest of sauce over liver, and bake, uncovered, for 10 minutes.   (Serves 4.)

> *To keep things cool in your picnic basket, fill*
> *small tightly sealed jars with ice cubes and place*
> *them near sandwiches and other food.*

DELICIOUS GRAVIES

4 tbsp. flour	Freshly ground pepper
2 to 4 tbsp. fat	1 tsp. salt
2 cups tomato OR other vegetable juice, vegetable water (cooled), soup stock or plain water	1/4 tsp. fresh herbs OR pinch dried herbs

Add flour to hot fat from roast and stir thoroughly.

Brown flour and fat to the colour desired over moderate heat, reduce heat and add the liquid slowly, stirring constantly.   Cool liquid prevents lumps.

Add seasonings and simmer for at least 10 minutes. You can, of course, shake the liquid and flour in a small sealed jar (or use blender) till it is smooth. Heat it and add meat juices and seasonings.

BEEF OR VEAL

Marjoram, rosemary, savory, basil, oregano, chives, onions, leeks, parsley, garlic, mustard, celery, caraway or cardamom seed, Worcestershire sauce, ketchup.

CHICKEN OR VEAL

Sage, savory, basil, thyme, marjoram, chives, leeks, canned or fresh pimiento, paprika.

LAMB

Like chicken gravy or combine chervil, rosemary, savory and marjoram. Or add 1 tsp. dill seed or fresh dill or 1 tbsp. capers.

PORK OR HAM

Sage, savory, dill, thyme, chives, parsley, garlic, minced leeks, celery or mustard seed. Ham is wonderful with mustard or caraway seed.

MARINADE FOR STEAKS

2 cloves garlic	1 tsp. curry powder
3 tbsp. salad OR olive oil	1 tsp. lime OR lemon juice
Dash of Angostura bitters	Salt and freshly ground pepper
Dash of Worcestershire sauce	(to taste)

Crush garlic into oil and add bitters, Worcestershire, curry powder and lime or lemon juice.

Marinate steak in this mixture for 3 to 4 hours, turning it once half-way through soaking period.

Broil or charcoal-grill the steak. Add salt and freshly ground pepper and pour remainder of marinade (heat it first) over steak.

Use a cork with cleanser to clean your chopping knives. It will protect fingers.

BARBECUE SAUCE

6 tbsp. butter
1 cup ketchup
4 tbsp. Worcestershire sauce
4 tbsp. meat extract
1 onion, stuck with 3 cloves
2 cloves garlic

1 cup water
1 tbsp. prepared mustard
1/2 tsp. salt
1/2 tsp. pepper
Tabasco (to taste)

Heat ingredients in a saucepan and bring to the boil, after which simmer for half an hour.   Remove onion.

Pass through a fine sieve, or blend in electric blender, return to saucepan and simmer for 10 minutes.   This sauce can be made in quantity because it keeps perfectly in the refrigerator for a month and 6 months in the freezer.

Spread it on steaks, hamburgers or pieces of chicken while they are broiling or cooking on outdoor barbecue.

HERB PASTE FOR STEAKS OR CHOPS

1 small onion
1 garlic clove
2 tsp. Worcestershire sauce
1/2 tsp. salt
Dash of cayenne

4 tbsp. parsley, chopped
1/4 tsp. rosemary
1/4 tsp. savory
5 tbsp. butter

Grate onion and garlic and add seasonings and the herbs which are finely minced. (Rub through fingers for fine effect.)

Cream with a wooden spoon, add butter and mix well.

Spread over surface of meat which has just been taken from pan or broiler.   Serve immediately.

Fowl and Game

When the price of red meat rises, many of us turn to chicken
and turkey and find numerous ways of changing their identity
for frequent use. The occasional gift of game, of course,
adds excitement to the menu. The clay pot is worth men-
tioning when we talk of roasting fowl or game as its great
feature is cooking without losing moisture — an important
point with all meats that dry out easily. If you cook a lot of
game, then reserve a clay pot just for that use as the unique
flavour of duck or goose may affect the flavour of tame meats
cooked in the same pot. However, the clay pot may be used
for chicken, turkey, lamb, ham, pork or veal. So many of
our good ways of game cookery came from the Indians while
other influences are distinctively European.

CHICKEN AND HAM CASSEROLE

2 stewing chickens (4 to 5 lb. each)
Few celery leaves
1 onion, sliced
1 tsp. salt
1/2 tsp. pepper
1/4 tsp. thyme
1 bay leaf
1 lb. mushrooms, sliced
3 tbsp. butter
1 1/2 lb. cooked ham
2 tbsp. onion, finely chopped
1/2 cup butter
3/4 cup flour
1 qt. rich milk
1 qt. chicken broth
2 tbsp. ketchup
1/4 tsp. dry mustard
2 tsp. salt
1 tsp. monosodium glutamate (MSG)
1/2 tsp. pepper
2 8-oz. pkgs. thin noodles
Slivered, toasted almonds (optional)

Cut up chickens and place in pot, with just enough water to cover.

Add celery leaves, sliced onion, salt, pepper, thyme and bay leaf. Cook slowly till a fork easily pierces the chicken. Let chicken cool in the broth.

Remove skin from chicken and take the meat from the bones. Cut into bite-size pieces.

Place the skin and bones back in the broth and simmer, covered, for 1 hour.

Strain, cool and skim off fat.

Sauté mushrooms in 3 tbsp. butter for 5 minutes.

Cut ham into small slices, and make a rich sauce as follows:

Melt 1/2 cup butter in a saucepan.

Add onion and cook a few minutes.

Stir in flour and blend.

Slowly add milk and strained chicken broth in which the chicken was cooked.

Cook until thick and smooth, stirring all the time.

Add ketchup, mustard, salt, monosodium glutamate, pepper.

Cook noodles according to directions on package. Drain and rinse in cold water.

Add noodles, ham, mushrooms and chicken to the sauce and pour into one or two casseroles. You may freeze one for future use.

Top with almonds and bake for 45 minutes in a 350-degree oven. (Serves 12 to 15.)

Note: This casserole can be made the day before and kept in the refrigerator. Bring to room temperature before baking.

CHICKEN PIE

1 4-to-5-lb. stewing chicken	1/2 cup butter OR chicken fat
1 stick celery	7 tbsp. flour
1 tbsp. parsley	1/2 tsp. pepper
1 large onion	1/4 tsp. mace
1 tbsp. salt	1/2 tsp. savory
1/4 tsp. dry mustard	1 tbsp. Worcestershire sauce
4 cups hot water	1 cup cream
12 small onions	3 cups chicken broth
Green peas and carrots (to taste)	1 pie crust OR biscuit topping

Place chicken, celery, parsley, large onion, salt, mustard, and hot water in a saucepan and bring to a boil. Skim, if necessary.

Cover and simmer over low heat for 3 or 4 hours or until chicken is tender.

Cool chicken and broth quickly, then remove meat from the bones. Place meat in a bowl and pour a cupful of broth on top. Cover and place in refrigerator until ready to use. Reserve remainder of broth.

Boil small onions until tender but not too soft (about 20 minutes). Drain and set aside. Prepare and cook as many peas and carrots as required. Or use tinned vegetables.

Melt butter or chicken fat, blend in flour and add pepper, mace, savory, Worcestershire sauce and cream. Stir together until well mixed.

Add chicken broth and cook over medium heat, stirring all the time, until smooth and creamy. Taste for seasoning.

Place chicken meat, onions, carrots and peas in a large casserole and pour the cream sauce over them. Arrange a pie crust or biscuit topping on top.

Bake in a 425-degree oven for 30 minutes or until nicely browned. (Serves 6.)

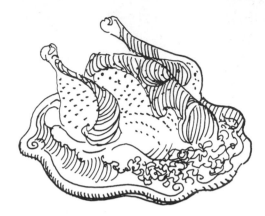

CHICKEN GALANTINE

1 chicken or boiling fowl
1/4 lb. bacon
2 tbsp. butter
1 tbsp. olive oil
1 bunch shallots (greens and
   whites), chopped
1/2 lb. mushrooms, thinly sliced
3 tbsp. parsley, finely chopped
1/4 tsp. thyme

1 bay leaf
1 tbsp. salt
1/2 tsp. pepper
1 clove garlic, crushed
3/4 cup boiling water (for each
   lb. of fowl)
1 tbsp. gelatin (for each 2 cups
   of broth)

Cook a chicken or boiling fowl in the following manner:
Melt bacon, cut into small pieces, together with butter and olive oil.

Add shallots and the fowl, cleaned and trussed. Cook until light gold.

Add mushrooms, parsley, thyme, bay leaf, salt, pepper, garlic and 3/4 cup of boiling water for each pound of fowl.

Cover and let simmer for 2 hours or until tender, reducing liquid to about 4 cups.

Bone and cut the meat into rather large pieces when fowl is tender and place in the warm broth. Add 1 tbsp. gelatin for each 2 cupfuls of broth.

Pour into a well-oiled mould and cool for 6 to 24 hours. (If desired, gelatin can be replaced by 2 or 3 lb. of veal knuckle cooked in the pot with the fowl.)

CHICKEN CASSEROLE SUISSE

1 4-to-6 lb. chicken or fowl	1 clove garlic, chopped finely
Flour mixed with a little salt	2 whole cloves
pepper, paprika and MSG	1/2 bay leaf
Butter	1/4 tsp. basil
1/2 cup white wine	1 cup Swiss cheese
1 cup water	Strained chicken stock
3 tbsp. parsley	2 tbsp. flour
2 shallots	1/4 cup cream

Cut chicken or fowl into individual portions. Roll in seasoned flour and brown in butter. Add wine and water (if wine is not to be used, add more water).

Flavour with parsley, shallots, clove of garlic, whole cloves, bay leaf and basil. Cover and simmer until bird is tender (around 50 minutes for a young bird, longer for an older one).

Grate cheese and butter a shallow casserole.

Strain stock from pan in which chicken has been cooking and measure 1 1/2 cups. If possible, remove 3 tbsp. fat from surface and place in a saucepan along with flour. Use butter if chicken fat can't be skimmed from stock. Combine thickened stock and cream, taste for seasoning.

Pour half of the sauce into casserole and sprinkle with half the grated cheese.

Arrange chicken on sauce and pour remainder of sauce over it and finish with a sprinkling of grated cheese. Keep at room temperature till ready to bake or store overnight in refrigerator, bringing to room temperature before placing in a 425-degree oven to bake for 30 minutes.

Professional chefs give this tip: keep a clean towel handy at all times for wiping hands while you're preparing food or mopping up.

CHICKEN VESUVIO

Louis Jaques, well-known photographer, and I ate this dish in New York's Vesuvio restaurant. Another recipe, also named after the volcano and found in several cookbooks, bears no resemblance to this dish. I serve it often to small dinner parties.

2 broilers or chicken-in-the-basket
2 cups soft bread crumbs
3/4 cup Parmesan cheese, grated
Salt and pepper

Few sprigs parsley, chopped
1 egg, beaten
Bacon strips (optional)
1/4 cup melted butter

Cut chicken into 2-inch pieces, breaking bones where necessary. If it is possible, and your butcher is willing to do the work, bone the broiler or chicken. Make a good consommé with the bones.

Combine crumbs, cheese, salt, pepper and parsley.

Dip pieces of chicken in beaten egg and roll each in crumb mixture.

Wrap strip of bacon around each piece of chicken and roll in small squares of wax-paper or foil, which have been spread lightly with melted butter. Fold ends over to seal.

Place in shallow baking dish or on baking sheet and bake at 400 degrees for 25 minutes. For crisper bacon, bake an extra 5-10 minutes or unwrap a little and place under broiler. If desired, cook without bacon.

Serve with herb bread and a good green salad. Remove chicken from paper wrappings or let each guest do his own. I serve Chicken Vesuvio in its wrappings in a large basket from which guests help themselves at table. (Serves 6.)

STEWED CHICKEN WITH CAPER SAUCE

1 4-to-5-lb. stewing chicken
2 tbsp. flour
1 tsp. salt
1/8 tsp. pepper
1 tsp. paprika
1/2 cup salad oil OR hot fat
1/4 cup capers OR diced pickles

2 cups water
1 tin undiluted cream of celery
  soup
1/2 tsp. curry powder
1/4 tsp. thyme
Dash of nutmeg

Cut chicken into individual pieces.

Shake flour, salt, pepper and paprika together in a paper bag. Place chicken in bag and shake well so that each piece is coated.

Brown slowly in salad oil or hot fat of your choice. Turn pieces as they brown.

Add water, celery soup, curry powder, thyme and nutmeg after all the pieces of chicken are browned.

Cook, covered, over low heat until chicken is tender (2 1/2 to 3 hours).

Place hot chicken in a serving dish and keep warm.

Measure broth and for each cup add 1 tablespoon of flour stirred until smooth with 2 tablespoons of cold water. Pour broth back in pan and cook until smooth and creamy, stirring constantly.

Add capers or diced pickles and the reserved pieces of chicken. Heat together for a few minutes and serve. (Serves 4 to 6.)

QUICK CHICKEN SAUTÉED

1 2 1/2-to-3-lb. broiler or young chicken, cut into individual pieces

Flour (seasoned with salt and pepper)

1/4 cup melted fat OR salad oil

1 can condensed cream of mushroom soup, undiluted

1/2 cup milk

1 medium-sized onion, sliced

1/2 tsp. thyme

Roll chicken in seasoned flour until well coated.

Brown in fat or salad oil, and when well browned on all sides, add mushroom soup.

Add milk and onion and sprinkle with thyme. Stir together until well mixed.

Cover and simmer for 30 minutes or longer over a medium heat, basting 3 or 4 times during cooking period. (Serves 4.)

Use a wooden spoon to spread fat thinly and evenly in a frying pan. Fat melts slower than on a metal spoon, making spreading easier.

BROILERS CORDON BLEU

3 broilers (1 1/2 to 2 lb. each)
OR roasting chickens, cut up
5 tbsp. butter
1 tsp. dry mustard
1/2 tsp. tarragon
Salt and pepper (to taste)

4-oz. red currant jelly
Juice of 1/2 lemon
1/2 cup water
3 whole cloves
1 tsp. salt
1/2 cup port wine (optional)
1 tbsp. cornstarch

Split broilers in two.

Cream 4 tbsp. butter with mustard and tarragon, and rub the skin of each broiler with this mixture. Salt and pepper to taste.

Place broilers in a dripping pan, buttered side up.

Roast for 20 minutes in a 450-degree oven. Lower heat to 325 degrees and cook another 20 to 25 minutes or until tender. Baste a few times during cooking period.

Make a sauce by combining 1 tbsp. butter, currant jelly, lemon juice, water, cloves and salt. Simmer and thicken with cornstarch that has been mixed with port wine or water. Stir constantly after adding cornstarch until sauce has a clear, creamy consistency.

Serve broilers with sauce. They are just as good served hot or cold with a hot or cold sauce. (Three broilers serve 6. If using roasting chicken, allow 1/2 lb. for each person.)

SKILLET CHICKEN LIVERS

This is one of our favourite Sunday morning dishes. I buy fresh chicken livers at chicken barbecue restaurants which are only too glad to get rid of them. I buy them in quantity and freeze them. It's an ideal recipe for serving to a brunch party.

18 chicken livers
1/4 cup butter
1 tbsp. parsley, chopped
8 mushrooms, chopped
1 tbsp. flour

1 cup of chicken stock OR consommé
1 small bay leaf
Pinch of thyme
Salt and pepper
Grilled bacon

Clean livers, wash in cold water and dry in a clean towel.

Cut each liver into three pieces (or more) and sauté over a very low flame in butter. Add parsley and mushrooms.

Sprinkle flour over liver. Blend well with wooden spoon, then add chicken stock or consommé, bay leaf and thyme.

Cover and simmer gently for 15 to 20 minutes, stirring occasionally.

Season with salt and pepper and a little grating of nutmeg. Serve on dry toast with two strips of grilled bacon for each portion. (Serves 6.)

(If this is to be served for supper, include green pepper and shallots with parsley and mushrooms. Use 1/2 cup of white wine if you have some and cut the amount of stock in half. A chicken bouillon cube in hot water makes an ideal stock.)

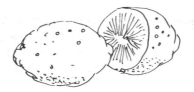

ITALIAN ROAST CHICKEN

2 very small roasting chickens
    or broilers
Half a lemon
1 clove of garlic, minced
2 tbsp. parsley, minced
Salt and pepper

2 green onions, minced
Chicken gizzard and liver, minced
1/2 tsp. minced or crushed rosemary
1/2 tsp. summer savory, crushed
Salad OR olive oil

Rub chickens inside and out with lemon. (Lemon keeps meat white and also cleans chicken.) Then rub chicken inside with a little oil on a piece of cheesecloth or wax-paper.

Combine garlic, parsley, salt and pepper, onions, gizzard and liver, rosemary and savory. (If you prefer any other herbs, they may be used. Simple poultry seasoning, thyme or basil will do as well.) Add oil to make a paste. The amount of oil depends on individual taste. I use about 4 tbsp.

Divide paste into 2 portions, putting half into the cavity of each bird. This does not fill the cavity but the flavouring permeates the whole bird beautifully.

Tie legs to the body, rub oil or butter on the outside of the birds, salt and pepper the skin and brown all over in an oiled pan in a 400-degree oven (about 10 to 15 minutes). Reduce heat to 300 degrees and roast until legs move freely.

Baste several times with liquid from bottom of pan and a mixture of 2 tbsp. melted butter and a little hot stock. If you have white wine use it instead of stock. (Serves 4 to 6.)

To make this a complete dinner in one pot, lay small peeled white onions and quartered raw, peeled potatoes around the chickens, salt and pepper them, and baste them each time the chickens are basted. Or place chickens on a heated platter and surround with hot, cooked noodles.

SAUTÉED CHICKEN

1 2 1/2-to-3-lb. broiler or young
chicken
3 to 4 tbsp. oil, butter OR bacon
dripping

Chopped parsley OR paprika
3 to 4 tbsp. apple juice, tomato
juice OR Canadian cider
Paprika OR flour, lightly seasoned

Cut chicken into individual pieces or quarters.
Heat oil, butter or bacon dripping in a large skillet.
Sprinkle chicken with paprika or roll in flour.
Brown quickly over medium heat on both sides.
Cover frying pan and allow chicken to cook slowly until tender. (Cooking time will vary from 25 to 60 minutes, depending on size of broiler or chicken used.)   Turn chicken occasionally as it cooks so that it will be a rich golden brown.
Uncover chicken during last 10 minutes of cooking so that it will have a crisper brown texture.
Sprinkle with parsley or paprika or any of your favourite herbs before removing from frying pan.
Add the liquid to the residue left in the pan and stir quickly over low heat.   Scrape the bottom of the pan to remove all the brown colour that has been stuck to it.
Pour this sauce over chicken.   (Serves 4.)

ORIENTAL CHICKEN PILAF

When I first published this recipe in the 50s, I said it would serve 8.   Now that I have three children, I have to alter that. This recipe will barely feed our family of two adults with normal appetites and three hungry children.

1/2 cup butter OR margarine
2 cups cooked chicken, cut into
strips about 1 1/2 inches long
1/4 cup onions, diced
2 tsp. salt
1/8 tsp. pepper
1/2 tsp. oregano or thyme

1 cup uncooked white rice
2 1/2 cups chicken stock OR 2 1/2
cups hot water and 2 chicken
bouillon cubes
1/2 cup chopped fresh or canned
tomatoes, drained
1/2 cup walnuts OR almonds,
chopped

135

Melt butter or margarine in a large saucepan.   Add chicken and onion and cook until onions are soft.   Add salt, pepper and oregano or thyme.

Add rice and cook, stirring occasionally, for 5 minutes. Slowly add chicken stock or water and bouillon cubes.

Add tomatoes and nuts, bring to a boil and cover and simmer 20 minutes or until rice is tender.   Do not stir.

Serve hot.

Note: Cook chicken the day before your party.   Save broth for soups. Increase amount of chicken, if desired.

THE CLAY POT

Cooking in an unglazed clay pot is healthy.   It is ideal for dieters or the heart-patient on a low sodium no-fat diet. The porosity of the unglazed clay allows the food to brown and take on an appetizing appearance and you do not have to add any fat or liquid to get fine results.   Ham, a loin of pork, a pot roast, a veal roast, chicken, whole or cut up — all can be cooked in the clay pot without the flavour from the previous meat being transferred.

ROAST CHICKEN

4-5 lb. roasting chicken	Pepper
2 leeks	Parsley
Sausages (optional)	

Wipe the chicken inside and out with a cut lemon or with a cloth rinsed out in vinegar.

Place in the pre-soaked clay pot.   Tuck washed leeks into the cavity, sprinkle with pepper and cover.   Roast in a 400-degree oven for 45 minutes.   The pot bastes the meat.

If desired, you may add sausages around the chicken and roast another 15-30 minutes, covered at the same temperature.

Pour out juices, remove fat, and make the gravy in a saucepan by thickening with a beurre-manié made by combining equal parts of flour and butter or margarine into a paste and dropping small dots into the hot mixture, stirring all the time.   Add salt, if desired.

ROAST TURKEY

Order your bird in advance or choose a fresh or frozen turkey. Choose a bird that's been drawn, pin feathers removed and cleaned all over.

Allow 1/2 to 3/4 lb. for each person. Remember the weight of the bird in order to regulate roasting time.

Frozen turkeys must be thawed as the label directs. If it is a frozen stuffed bird, it can be placed in the oven without thawing. It takes 2 to 3 days for a large bird to thaw in the refrigerator. Thawing is hastened if the giblets are removed as soon as the cavity is partially thawed.

Make stuffing in advance and refrigerate. It is wiser to stuff the bird on the day it is to be roasted, but I have stuffed large birds a day in advance and kept them very cold overnight without unhappy results.

Stuff neck first and fold over skin, securing it with a skewer.

Rub interior of turkey with monosodium glutamate and salt (or lemon halves which help to whiten meat.) Fill with favourite stuffing and close body opening with poultry pins or skewers. Lace cavity with string or twine and wind around legs, drawing the legs together and putting final knot under the tail.

Brush skin with salad oil or a mixture of soft butter and dry mustard.

Roast turkey, breast up, on a wire rack in an uncovered roasting pan.

Moisten a large piece of clean cheesecloth with soft fat, place over top and sides of bird and, from time to time, ladle fat from the pan over the cloth to keep it moist.

Before roasting is completed, cut string between legs. When drumsticks move easily up and down, remove bird to heated platter, keep in a warm place and make the gravy.

Roast at 325 degrees. A 10-lb. bird takes 4 to 5 hours. A 20-lb. bird takes approximately 7 1/2 to 8 1/2 hours. A smaller bird takes from 3 to 4 1/2 hours. It is a good idea to buy a cooking thermometer and stick it into the bird in the thigh muscle adjoining the body. It will read 190 degrees when the turkey is cooked.

FLUFFY STUFFING

14 cups white bread crumbs
   or cubes
2 tsp. poultry seasoning OR mixed
   thyme, marjoram, sage and
   tarragon
4 tsp. salt

1 tsp. pepper
1/4 to 1/2 cup minced onion
2 cups diced celery
1 to 2 cups giblet broth OR water
1 cup butter OR margarine

Thoroughly combine bread crumbs, poultry seasoning or mixture of thyme, marjoram, sage and tarragon, salt, pepper, minced onion, diced celery.

Add just enough giblet broth or water and butter to moisten bread crumbs slightly (not enough to make soggy mixture). Bread should be moistened, not saturated.

Mix well and use to stuff a 20-lb. turkey.

POTATO STUFFING

Turkey heart, gizzard and liver
3 onions
1/2 to 1-lb. minced pork
8 to 10 potatoes
4 tbsp. turkey fat OR butter

1/2 to 1 tsp. savory
1 tbsp. salt
1/4 tsp. pepper
1 tsp. dry mustard

Mince turkey heart, gizzard and liver. Chop onions.

Combine minced pork, heart, gizzard and liver.

Boil potatoes leaving the skins on. Peel and mash.

Meanwhile, melt turkey fat or butter in a large frying pan (takes 10 to 15 minutes to melt turkey fat).

Add onions and fry lightly. Add giblets and pork. Stir in fat over high heat until rawness disappears. Add seasonings.

Add potatoes to meat mixture and beat until well mixed. Add more salt if necessary.

Cool, before using to stuff turkey.

A good way to measure herbs is to dip your little finger into the herb bottle. What you can hold on the end of your finger will be the right amount to add to a dish serving six to eight persons.

CORNFLAKE AND WALNUT STUFFING

Giblets
2 cups water
4 cups bread cubes, toasted
8 cups cornflakes
1/2 cup minced parsley
3 onions, chopped
2 cups celery, diced

1 cup walnuts, minced
2 tsp. salt
1 tsp. pepper
1/2 tsp. monosodium glutamate
  (MSG)
2 tsp. savory OR sage
3/4 cup milk
2 eggs, well beaten

Cook giblets in water, covered, over medium heat until tender (about 1 hour).

Combine in a large bowl bread cubes, cornflakes, parsley, onions, celery, walnuts, salt, pepper, monosodium glutamate and savory or sage.

Beat milk and eggs together and add to mixture.

Mix and add chopped giblets and 1/2 cup of the giblet water.

Mix and chill for 1 hour to blend flavours.   (Stuffs a 10-to-12-lb. turkey.)

CASSEROLE DUCK À L'ORANGE

1 duck, domestic or wild	1 tsp. salt
3 tbsp. butter	1/2 tsp. pepper
Grated rind of 1 orange	Duck liver, chopped
1/2 cup orange juice	1/2 cup water, apple juice OR
1/4 tsp. cinnamon	orange juice
1/4 tsp. cloves	1 tsp. cornstarch

Cut duck into individual pieces. (The average duck usually serves only two.)

Melt butter in a heavy casserole and brown pieces of duck all over.

Add grated rind of 1 orange, 1/2 cup of orange juice, cinnamon, cloves, salt and pepper and stir well.

Cover and cook over low heat until duck is tender (about 1 1/2 hours). Use clay baker if desired.

Remove duck, when cooked, to a warm dish. Add chopped liver and water, or apple or orange juice which has been mixed with cornstarch. Cook a few minutes to remove raw starch taste and pour over duck.

Cool, and about half an hour before eating, reheat slowly. This is delicious with cooked wild or brown rice to which a couple of tablespoons of chutney have been added. A green salad, to which segments of fresh or canned oranges have been added, is another accompaniment.

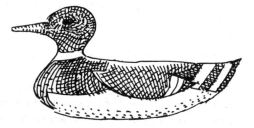

DUCK À L'ORANGE

1 duck, domestic or wild
Duck liver
Grated rind of 1/2 orange
1/4 tsp. cinnamon
1/4 tsp. cloves

Salt and pepper
3 tbsp. butter
1 tsp. dry mustard
Juice of 1/2 orange
Oranges, thinly sliced

Clean duck and chop liver.

Add grated rind of 1/2 orange, cinnamon and cloves to liver. Salt and pepper the interior of the duck, and place liver mixture in cavity.

Place duck in dripping pan without a rack. Mix butter, mustard and juice of 1/2 orange together and spread this paste over the duck.

Place orange slices on buttered breast.

Roast in a 350-degree oven for 20 minutes to the pound, or roast in a clay baker.

DUCK AND SAUERKRAUT

1 4-to-5-lb. domestic duck
Salt
Pepper
Marjoram
2 apples, unpeeled
2 chestnuts, peeled (optional)

2 large tins sauerkraut
2 onions, chopped
1/2 cup pineapple chunks
Paprika
Water
1 tsp. sugar

Rub duck with salt, pepper and marjoram and fill cavity with apples. (If chestnuts are available include them with apple stuffing.)

Roast duck in a 350-degree oven for 1 1/2 to 2 hours, or till tender.

Drain off most of fat in pan, brown sauerkraut in remaining fat, add onions, pineapple, salt , pepper and paprika. Cook, stirring over quick heat, till sauerkraut is a rich brown.

Add a little water and the sugar and simmer till sauerkraut is tender and liquid has evaporated.

Before serving with duck, a cup of dry white wine may be poured over the sauerkraut. It gives it a delicious flavour.

PARTRIDGE IN THE VINE

1 small partridge per person
Lemon juice
Salt and pepper
Ground cloves

Ginger
2 bacon slices for each partridge
Grape leaves OR cabbage leaves

Rub each cleaned, plucked bird with lemon juice, salt and pepper.

Sprinkle lightly with cloves and ginger and wrap in bacon slices.

Place in a shallow roasting pan and cover with grape or cabbage leaves (Greek grocers import grape leaves, or you can take the very tiny leaves from your own grape vine).

Roast in a 400-degree oven for about 20 minutes, remove leaves and bacon.

Increase heat to 450 degrees, baste the birds with the juice (add a little red wine for flavour if desired) and brown them.

To serve, sprinkle with browned, buttered bread crumbs and decorate with fresh leaves or parsley.

VENISON IN THE POT

1 roast venison, lamb OR mutton
3 tbsp. flour
1 tbsp. paprika
1 tsp. rosemary OR sage
1 sour apple, grated and unpeeled

1/2 cup minced beef suet
1/4 cup olive oil
1 tsp. salt
1/2 cup light red wine

Roll the roast in a mixture of flour, paprika, rosemary or sage.

Melt minced beef suet or heat olive oil in a heavy saucepan. Brown the meat slightly all around in the melted fat, sprinkle with salt and add wine and apple.

Cover the pan and allow to cook slowly, turning once during the cooking, until the meat is tender (which can vary depending on the type of meat being cooked, but usually it will take from 1 1/2 to 2 hours of very slow cooking).

When the venison is served hot, it is always presented with the sauce remaining in the bottom of the saucepan. Serve sliced very thinly.

MOCK VENISON STEW

Even the hunters don't know that this is beef. Some people don't like game but they won't complain about this very good imitation of the real thing.

1 cup red wine OR 1 cup
   apple juice
1 onion, chopped finely
1 carrot, sliced
1 clove garlic
1/2 tsp. salt
3 peppercorns
2 whole cloves
1 bay leaf
1/2 tsp. thyme

2 to 3 lb. bottom or top round
   of beef, cut in 2-inch pieces
4 tbsp. flour
1/2 tsp. salt
1 tsp. paprika
1/4 cup dripping OR butter
1 large onion, chopped
2 tbsp. parsley, minced
1 tbsp. brown sugar
18 small onions (optional)

Place wine or apple juice, 1 onion, carrot, garlic, 1/2 tsp. salt, peppercorns, cloves, bay leaf and thyme in a large earthenware or glass bowl.

Add beef, cover and place in the refrigerator from 6 to 12 hours, turning the meat a few times. Drain the meat from mixture. Strain and reserve liquid.

Roll each piece of meat in flour which has been mixed with 1/2 tsp. salt and paprika, until well coated.

Brown the meat over quick heat in hot dripping or butter. Add 1 large onion, parsley and the strained liquid mixture used to soak the meat. Bring to a boil and add brown sugar.

Cover and simmer over low heat until meat is tender (about 30 minutes).

Cook the 18 small onions in a separate pan and add to the gravy when ready to serve, or onions may be omitted.

Serve with boiled rice and cabbage or broccoli.

(Serves 6.)

Peppercorns should be crushed before going into soups and stews, to let the oils escape into the food. A good way to do this is to put them in a clean towel and crush with an ordinary hammer.

RABBIT STEW

I cooked my first rabbit for artist Carlo Italiano and his wife, Marilyn, two delightful people who live in the country and claim they catch wild game in their garden. No, I don't believe Carlo eats robins but I believe he is one of the most appreciative eaters I know — and one of the finest artists.

1 rabbit, wild or domestic	1 cup wine vinegar
2 bacon slices	1 cup water
4 tbsp. butter	3 tbsp. oil
1 cup onions, sliced	2 bay leaves
1 or 2 tbsp. flour	1 tsp. pepper
Salt and pepper	1 tsp. thyme
1 1/2 cups of broth OR consommé	1 tsp. cloves
2/3 cup white wine (optional)	1/2 cup onions, finely minced
2 tsp. tarragon	or ground
1 tsp. basil	

Make a marinade of the last 8 ingredients.

Place the rabbit, cut into serving pieces, in it and marinate at least 6 hours for a younger animal.   Turn frequently.

Wipe pieces of rabbit and throw away the marinade.

Fry the bacon, remove from pan, add butter and cook onions till golden, remove them and sauté rabbit in the fat.

Add 1 or 2 tbsp. of flour, stir well and season to taste.

Add broth or consommé, wine (if wine is not used, increase the amount of broth by about 1/3 cup), tarragon, basil, cooked onions and bacon.

Simmer gently for 1 1/4 hours or till rabbit is tender.

Skim the fat from gravy before serving with the meat.

Eat with wild or brown rice and a red cabbage salad.

Fish

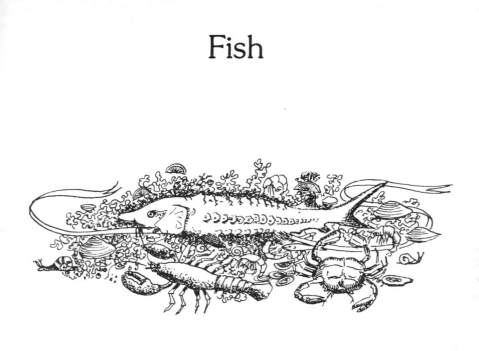

This is a small collection of recipes from my days with
Weekend Magazine. Since then I have collected many
more sea-food recipes and I plan to do a little book just
on fish later on.

I grew up in central Canada, before the freezer was standard
kitchen equipment, and so I was not exposed to the pleasures
of sea-food. I learned to love fish as an adult, and now, like
many inland Canadians, I appreciate it when fresh fish comes
my way.

PARTY LOBSTER

3 cups water
4 tbsp. lemon juice
1/2 tsp. salt
4 lobster tails, fresh or frozen
3 tbsp. butter
2 tbsp. flour
1/2 cup sherry (optional)

1/4 tsp. dry mustard
1/2 tsp. salt
1 cup sour cream (commercial type)
2 cups cooked rice
1/4 cup grated Swiss cheese
1/2 cup fine bread crumbs

Boil water, add lemon juice and salt. Add lobster tails, reduce heat and cook gently for 15 minutes. Do not overcook.

Crack shells and remove meat. Cool, then slice with sharp knife. Reserve liquid in which tails were cooked.

Melt butter in saucepan, blend in flour, add 1 cup of liquid in which lobster was cooked, then add sherry, mustard and salt. Turn off heat and then blend in sour cream.

Add lobster meat, but don't stir so hard that meat breaks.

Butter a casserole and spread a layer of cooked rice on the bottom. Pour lobster and sauce over rice and sprinkle with grated cheese, which has been mixed with bread crumbs. Dot with butter. Keep in refrigerator till an hour before food is to be served.

Remove from refrigerator and allow to come to room temperature (about 30 to 40 minutes), then bake at 400 degrees for 15 to 20 minutes or till crumbs are golden. (Serves 6.)

DEVILLED SEAFOOD

2 lb. haddock fillets, fresh or
  frozen
1 lb. lobster meat, cooked (canned
  or frozen)
8 tbsp. butter
4 to 5 tbsp. flour
1 cup evaporated milk OR cream
1 1/2 cups milk
1 tbsp. lemon juice
1 tbsp. Worcestershire sauce
4 tbsp. ketchup

1 tbsp. horseradish
1 clove garlic, grated
1 tsp. prepared mustard
1/2 tsp. salt
1 tsp. soy sauce
1 tsp. monosodium glutamate
  MSG
4 tbsp. parsley, minced
Fine bread crumbs
Dots of butter

Grease the inside of the top of a double boiler and place over boiling water. (If fish is frozen, cover with salted cold water and let stand in water for 15 minutes, then drain. This is not necessary if you are using fresh fish.)

Put haddock in double boiler and cover. Steam for 20 minutes. When cool, separate fish into bite-sized pieces.

Separate lobster into small pieces.

Melt butter and blend in flour.

Heat evaporated milk or cream with fresh milk and pour slowly into flour and butter, stirring constantly.

Cook until thick, in top of a double boiler.

Add cornstarch, which has been blended with a little cold milk, and cook 10 minutes longer.

Add lemon juice, Worcestershire sauce, ketchup, horse-radish, garlic, mustard, salt, soy sauce and Ac'cent.

Mix and stir in parsley and sherry. When thoroughly mixed add fish and lobster and pour into a greased casserole.

Sprinkle top with fine bread crumbs and dots of butter and bake for 1/2 hour in a 400-degree oven. (Serves 10.)

Note: This casserole can be prepared the day before and stored in the refrigerator. Bring to room temperature before baking.

POACHED CANADIAN SALMON

Let the Irish and the Scots talk of their salmon; we in Canada have both Atlantic and Pacific varieties to choose from and they are our pride. It's a great dish to serve visitors from Europe incidentally, because it's such an expensive rarity there. While it's true that the initial outlay is considerable for a whole salmon, I think it's good economy since you get so many interesting meals from it. I prefer to poach mine because it makes an impressive appearance on the table. Buy a 6-10 lb. salmon and cook it in Court Bouillon in the following way:

COURT BOUILLON

Water to cover fish
2 cups dry white wine OR
  juice of 2 lemons
Sea salt OR regular kind
Fresh dill

1 onion, sliced
1 celery stalk, cut up
1 carrot, in 2 pieces
Handful of fresh parsley

Have fish cleaned and remove gills. It does not have to be scaled if it is to be served whole.

To make Court Bouillon (the best liquid to poach your salmon in), bring water to the boil with wine, 1 tbsp. salt per two quarts of water, several sprigs of fresh dill, onion, celery, carrot and parsley.

Simmer for 20 minutes, then remove from heat and bring to room temperature. Place fish in poacher, curling tail around if it is too long, or use a turkey roaster with lid, or a wash boiler (not galvanized, please) and strain Court Bouillon over it.

Bring to the boil then reduce heat immediately so that the fish does not boil. (You may have to remove pan from the heat till it is low again.) The water should "mijote" but not move - "barely simmer" is the best description. If you keep the water at this temperature your salmon will be cooked in 1 1/2 hours for a fish which is 5-10 pounds. A good rule is to allow 10 minutes per inch, measured at its widest spot.

When you remove it from the heat, you may leave it in the Court Bouillon for several hours before garnishing. If it is to be served hot, it may stay in the liquid because it won't lose its heat for some time.

My favourite way of serving poached salmon is to remove the skin, tuck a small daisy or other flower in the eye cavity, place it on a large oval platter (in desperation, you can use a clean piece of wood) and use a variety of garnishes — fresh dill, parsley, watercress, lettuce, radish roses, tomatoes and lemons cut in half — use a small knife and cut a serrated edge around the outside, cucumbers, devilled eggs, marinated artichoke hearts, small bouquets of cooked, marinated green beans, carrot strips.

Serve with mayonnaise combined with whipped cream or sour cream; or whipped cream mixed with a little hot dog mustard (yes, that's what I mean) or blend a cup of mayonnaise with a handful of fresh spinach, parsley, mint, fresh herb such as basil or tarragon to make a sauce verte.

It helps to have fish servers but it isn't difficult to serve a whole salmon. Using a spoon and fork, remove neat pieces from either side of the bone which runs along the middle of the flat side. When the top layer of salmon has been eaten, remove the whole fish backbone and you still have a whole layer to enjoy. Remove this side from the skin when serving.

SWEDISH CURED SALMON

I have been introduced to many delightful dishes via a Swedish friend, Peggy Gruman, a marvellous cook whose parties are famous. This is an unusual way to add variety to salmon. You can buy a three-pound piece from the middle or you can buy a whole fish, poach the tail piece, cut off steaks from the head and save the middle portion for the best imitation of smoked salmon I've ever come across.

1 3-lb. centre piece salmon	1 tsp. coarsely cracked black peppercorns
3 tbsp. sea salt	2 bunches fresh dill
1 tbsp. sugar	

Slit salmon with a sharp knife along the back and divide into two flat pieces. Remove the backbone and the little bones, feeling about with the fingers in order to get them all. Leave the skin on.

Combine salt and sugar.

Place a bed of dill in a shallow glass or pottery dish (not metal) and lay a layer of salmon on top. Rub salt and sugar over piece on both sides. Sprinkle pepper over cut side and rub second piece all over with sugar and salt. Sprinkle with pepper. Lay a generous amount of dill on bottom piece, place second piece of salmon on top, skin side up. Rub any remaining spices over it and cover with lots of dill.

Place a board on top and refrigerate for 24 hours or longer.

When ready to serve, scrape off spices and slice very thin on the bias. Serve with capers, brown bread and any of the sauces suggested for poached salmon.

SHRIMP MEUNIÈRE

2 cloves garlic, diced	1/4 cup olive oil
1/2 tsp. salt	2 lb. raw shelled shrimps
3 peppercorns	2 tbsp. lemon juice
1/4 cup melted butter	1 tbsp. parsley, cut finely

Crush garlic, salt and peppercorns in a skillet.
Add butter and olive oil, and heat.
Add shrimps and cook gently for about 5 minutes, or until done, stirring once or twice.
Add lemon juice and sprinkle with parsley.   (Serves 3 or 4.)

SEAFOOD CASSEROLE FOR A BUFFET SUPPER

This is a good item for a buffet meal because it may be prepared in advance, except for combining the sauce with the other ingredients.   This recipe calls for mushroom sauce. One can use mushroom soup or creamed mushrooms, but I find the following just as simple.   I melt 2-3 tbsp. butter, add a few chopped shallots, a crushed garlic clove and a dozen or more thinly sliced mushrooms.   I stir these around a bit, add milk or cream and sherry and cook just long enough to combine all the ingredients.

Line a greased casserole with 2 inches of drained, cooked rice (hot or cold).
Spread fresh or canned cooked seafood on top of the rice (shrimp, lobster, crab, tuna or a combination is ideal). Sprinkle with a pinch of tarragon, basil, parsley or celery flakes (or all four, if desired).
Top with mushroom sauce.   Do not stir.
Sprinkle buttered crumbs over casserole and bake, uncovered, in a 375-degree oven for 35 minutes.   Garnish with parsley, watercress or pimiento.

Cooked rice that is glutinous can be saved. Rinse it in your hands under the cold water tap. Kernels will separate and can be reheated.

SEAFOOD COCKTAIL

1 cup cooked shrimp, cleaned
1/2 cup lobster meat, diced
1/2 cup crab meat, flaked
1/4 cup tomato ketchup
1/2 cup chili sauce
1 tbsp. Worcestershire sauce
2 tbsp. lemon juice

1 tbsp. tarragon vinegar
1 tbsp. onion, minced
2 tbsp. celery, minced
1 tsp. grated horseradish
1/4 tsp. salt
3 dashes Tabasco sauce

Combine ketchup, chili sauce, Worcestershire sauce, lemon juice, vinegar, minced vegetables, horseradish and salt in a bowl.

Correct seasoning and add Tabasco sauce. Cover and chill.

Line chilled glasses or dishes with a lettuce leaf, arrange a layer of seafood over lettuce and spoon remainder of the sauce over it. Serve at once. (Serves 6 to 8.)

GREEK HADDOCK

Fresh tomatoes, thickly sliced
   OR 2 cups well-drained canned
   tomatoes
1/2 tsp. sugar
3 to 4 tbsp. minced fresh parsley
1 1/2 to 2 lb. haddock

1/4 cup salad oil
2 tbsp. flour
1 tsp. paprika
1 tsp. salt
Pinch of pepper

Cover bottom of a baking pan with a layer of tomatoes. Sprinkle tomatoes with sugar and parsley.

Place haddock on tomatoes.

Mix salad oil, flour, paprika, salt and pepper, and pour over the fish.

Bake in a 400-degree oven for 20 minutes.

TROUT CATCH

Fresh trout
7 slices unpeeled lemon
Salt and pepper

Steak sauce OR chutney
3 slices bacon
2 cups shredded lettuce

Skin and dry fresh trout and place 3 lemon slices in the cavity.

Sprinkle top of fish with salt and pepper and a small quantity of steak sauce or chutney.

Roll slices of bacon around trout.

Cover the bottom of baking dish with shredded lettuce and 4 lemon slices.

Place the trout on this green bed.

Cook in a 425-degree oven for 5 minutes for a 1-pound trout. (Serves 1.)

Note: A good way of judging the time to cook a fish is to allow 5 minutes for every inch of thickness at its thickest part. Allow 5 minutes to the pound if you know the weight. A tablespoon of sherry or brandy may be poured over the trout while it's cooking.

BAKED FILLET OF SOLE

2 lb. fillet of sole
2 tbsp. butter OR oil
1 cup soft bread crumbs
1/2 cup Parmesan cheese
Thyme (to taste)

Parsley, minced (to taste)
Salt and pepper
1 to 2 tbsp. olive oil, melted
   butter OR margarine
Paprika

Butter or oil a piece of aluminum foil. Sprinkle with a mixture of bread crumbs, grated cheese, thyme and parsley, salt and pepper. Place fish on this.

Drizzle a little olive oil, melted butter or margarine over fish and bake in a 350-degree oven for 15 to 20 minutes, or till fish flakes easily.

Sprinkle with more minced parsley and paprika and serve immediately. (Serves 6.)

DORÉ PIERRE OF THE RITZ

A book of Canadian recipes would not be complete without a contribution from Chef Pierre Demers of the Ritz Carlton Hotel in Montreal. Two of his fish dishes have become my favourites at home and Pierre has given me permission to pass them on to you. Chef Pierre, the most approachable cook I know, was the first Canadian-born chef to achieve international renown.

1 tbsp. butter	1 large or 2 small fresh tomatoes
1 tbsp. chopped French	4 fresh mushroom caps, sliced
shallots OR 1 tbsp.	Salt and pepper
Spanish or red onion	4 oz. dry white wine
2 6-oz. fillets of doré	1 cup 35 percent cream
(pickerel)	Chopped parsley

Butter a shallow oven dish which will also go on top of the stove. Sprinkle chopped onion over bottom and place fish fillets side by side on top. If you are increasing this recipe, use a dish large enough to allow fillets to be arranged in a single layer — or use more than one dish.

Arrange tomatoes, which have been peeled, seeded and sliced, over fish.

Sprinkle mushrooms over all and salt and pepper to taste.

Pour white wine over, then add cream.

Bring to boil on top of stove, cover with lid or piece of aluminum foil and bake in a 350-degree oven for 8-10 minutes. Do not boil too long or overbake.

Transfer fish to warmed serving plates, reduce liquid in dish over high heat to 2/3 of its original quantity, pour over fish and sprinkle with parsley. (Serves 2.)

Use aluminum foil over and over again by wiping it with a clean, damp sponge. Wiping removes wrinkles and cleans the foil.

PIERRE'S CANADIAN BOUILLABAISSE

By no means an economy dish, this is still worth trying. It's a spectacular party dish for a small dinner — and though Pierre probably wouldn't serve it reheated, I find it's still delicious for family eating one or two days later.

1 1/2 cups carrots, in fine
    julienne strips
1 1/2 cups leeks, in fine
    julienne strips
1 1/2 cups celery, in fine
    julienne strips
1 onion, cut fine
2-5 garlic cloves, chopped
8 canned tomatoes, squeezed dry
    in the hand
Parsley
2-3 threads of saffron OR
    powdered saffron
1 sprig of thyme
Tarragon, fresh, dried or marin-
    ated in vinegar or white wine

Spurt of brandy
1/2 bottle (13 oz.) dry white
    wine
1 1/2 quarts fish or chicken stock
    OR water
Sea salt or plain salt
White pepper
2 uncooked lobsters
4 slices of salmon from the tail,
    skin on
4 slices of halibut from the tail,
    skin on OR any firm fish such
    as doré, pike, trout
Handful of scallops
2 tbsp. butter, twice
1/3 cup oil, twice

This recipe, in spite of its length, isn't complicated.

Gather all your ingredients together.

Heat butter and oil in a large sauteuse or frying pan till hot, add vegetables, except for tomatoes and sauté till golden. Shake the pan frequently and stir with a wooden spoon for a few minutes.

Add saffron, stir and cook, then add coarsely chopped tomatoes, pepper, wine and stock or water.

Place uncooked fish slices in bottom of a large, deep Dutch Oven (preferably enamelled iron). Cut heads off fresh, uncooked lobsters and discard. Break off claws and cut body into four or five pieces, leaving the shell on.

Heat second 2 tbsp. butter and 1/3 cup oil till nutty, then add lobster pieces, stirring till shell turns bright pink.

Remove from fire and add brandy and salt, to taste. You may flame it if you wish but remember always to flame away from the heat. Place lobster over raw fish pieces.

Taste vegetables for salt and pepper and pour over fish.

Sprinkle with parsley and leave covered at room temperature a few hours till ready to cook. Chilling it spoils the fresh flavour.

Bring to a boil when ready to serve and cook gently for 25 minutes.

To serve, ladle out the broth and eat it separately if desired. Or simply ladle broth and fish into a wide-mouthed soup bowl. Eat with garlic croutons and follow with fresh fruit and hot coffee.

To make very good bread accompaniment, slice French bread very thin (if you spread the outside edge with butter first, it is very easy to slice thinly) and spread with a mixture of butter, garlic and chopped parsley. Toast in a 375-degree oven till crisp and golden. (Serves 4 generously.)

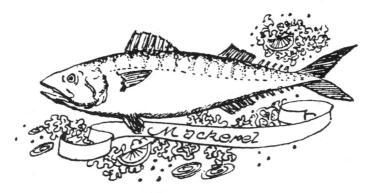

TENDER BROWN SCALLOPS

Fresh or frozen scallops can be used here. I use them fresh when I can get them.

1/2 tsp. salt	1 egg
Few grains pepper	2 tbsp. water
Few grains cayenne	1 1/2 lb. scallops
1 cup crumbs	4 tbsp. melted butter

Mix salt, pepper, cayenne and crumbs together.

Beat egg and water with a fork and dip each scallop first in crumbs, then egg mixture and again in crumbs.

Put in medium baking dish and let stand for about 30 minutes for coating to set.

Set oven at 450 degrees. Pour melted butter over scallops and bake 25 to 30 minutes or until scallops are nicely brown and crisp on the outside.

Serve with Tartar Sauce (recipe follows). (Serves 4.)

TARTAR SAUCE

1 dill pickle	1/2 small onion
1 tbsp. capers	1 cup mayonnaise
3 sprigs parsley	1 1/2 tbsp. prepared mustard

Chop pickle, capers, parsley and onion as finely as possible.

Mix mayonnaise and mustard.

Add chopped ingredients.

FISH FILLETS IN TOMATO SAUCE

1 1/2 to 2 lb. fish fillets, fresh OR
   frozen
Salt and pepper
1/4 tsp. sage
1/4 cup salad oil

2 medium-sized onions, thinly
   sliced
1 8-oz. tin tomato sauce
1/2 tsp. sugar

Cut fillets into individual portions (if using frozen fillets be sure to thaw them first.)

Roll each fillet and place in an oblong baking dish, one next to the other. Sprinkle with salt, pepper and sage.

Fry onions in salad oil and add tomato sauce and sugar. Season to taste, then bring to a boil and pour over fish.

Bake for 15 minutes in a 425-degree oven.

Serve with green peas and mashed potatoes.

(Serves 5 to 6.)

FISH IN COURT BOUILLON

Any whole fish can be cooked in Court Bouillon. If you're using fish other than salmon, you may prefer to use vinegar or white wine instead of lemon juice and serve the fish with egg sauce.

EGG SAUCE

2 tbsp. butter
2 tbsp. flour
1/2 tsp. salt
1/8 tsp. pepper
1 cup scalded milk OR cream

1 hard-cooked egg
1 tsp. minced parsley
1/4 tsp. curry
1 tbsp. mayonnaise

Melt butter, add flour and blend thoroughly.

When smooth, add salt and pepper and, lastly, scalded milk or cream.

Stir constantly over low heat until thickened. Never brown it. Cook 5 minutes.

Add egg, either sliced or crushed, parsley, curry and mayonnaise.

FISHERMAN'S CODFISH CAKES

1 lb. salt codfish
8 potatoes
2 large onions

Salt and pepper (to taste)
Pinch of sugar
Salad oil OR cooking fat

Shred codfish. Place in cold water and bring to a boil. (Do not boil after fish has been added to water.) Repeat this procedure 3 times, using fresh water each time.
Boil potatoes in salted water.
Sauté onions until they are a deep brown.
Beat codfish, potatoes and onion together and add salt. pepper and sugar. The mixture should be fairly soft.
Mix into patties and fry in oil or fat until they are a golden or deep brown colour. (Serves 4.)

FISH MULLIGAN

3 strips bacon, sliced
3 onions, sliced and peeled
1 1/2 lb. fresh or frozen cod
    OR haddock fillets
1 1/2 lb. potatoes, pared and
    cubed
1/2 tsp. celery seed

3 large carrots, pared and cubed
1/4 cup green peppers, diced
1 1/2 tsp. salt
1/4 tsp. pepper
3 cups boiling water
1 large can tomatoes (3 1/2 cups)
2 tbsp. minced parsley

Brown bacon lightly in a deep pot or Dutch Oven.
Remove bacon and set aside. Brown onions in bacon fat till golden.
Cut fish into 2-inch pieces and add with potatoes, celery seed, carrots, green peppers, salt and pepper.
Add boiling water and simmer, covered, till vegetables are tender — about 20 minutes.
Add tomatoes and heat. Do not boil.
Garnish with parsley and the bacon. (Serves 6.)

Vegetables

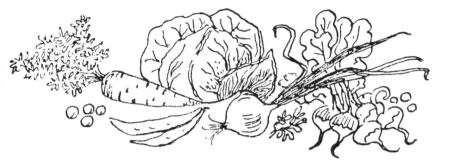

I think we are more health conscious than we were twenty years ago. We are concerned with vitamins and conservation and ecology, and it is no longer true that "we show little respect for vegetables in this country where icing a cake gets more attention than the conservation of vitamins in the vegetable pot." There are also many more vegetarians among us, and growing vegetables on the balcony or in the backyard is as fashionable as flower gardening.

Like soup making, the cooking of vegetables is a test of your ability and common sense. For vegetables the first rule is always to undercook rather than overcook. After all, any vegetable can be eaten raw. Pressure cookers are still favoured by many for the cooking of vegetables, but I lean toward the steamer basket that fits into any size pot because of its collapsible sides and feet. For vegetables such as broccoli, I use the French method in which vegetables are plunged into boiling water and boiled furiously just long enough to soften the stalks but not enough to remove the colour. I have lately cooked vegetables in the microwave oven and been happy with the results.

The best way to really appreciate vegetables is to have your own garden. A green bean or stalk of asparagus grown in Texas is a poor and distant cousin to the one picked in your own patch and cooked without delay. I also prefer frozen vegetables to the wilted ones found on the grocer's shelves during winter months. Frozen vegetables cook beautifully in the steamer basket. As for canned vegetables, l have a select few on the shelf, too — Italian pear tomatoes with a basil leaf, French green beans packed in tidy, slim clusters, creamed corn, rosebud beets, tiny sweet peas, zucchini, small carrots, European haricot beans and chick peas.

Chefs who took part in my CBC-TV series "Bon Appetit" let me in on many of their professional tricks. They cook, let's say, broccoli, hours ahead till it's beautifully Irish green and slightly tender, then drain and transfer it to a serving dish, cover it with parchment or wax-paper and keep it in a cool place till ready to eat. At serving time, they add butter and heat very quickly until the vegetables are warm. I have done this with green beans, carrots, asparagus, spinach, cabbage, cauliflower and peas and found it simplified my evening meal, which very often has to be put together in a hurry.

Some vegetables combine, gastronomically and visually, better than others. Cauliflower and potatoes, for example, need a strong colour contrast. Added touches to cooked vegetables can include herbs, seasoned salt, French dressing, sour cream, yogurt, curry, melted butter, MSG, chives, chopped onion, garlic, paprika, nutmeg, cheese and mint. It's a good idea not to cook more vegetables than you need for the meal unless you want them for soup. Vegetables heated a day later aren't that good. However, potatoes can be cooked in their skins and stored for re-use without any loss of vitamins. Where possible, scrub vegetables rather than peel them, don't soak them for long periods before cooking and slice, sliver or shred them if you aren't going to cook them whole.

MASHED POTATOES À L'ITALIENNE

Potatoes and cheese have an affinity. If you have a blender, it comes in handy to make use of left-over odds and ends of cheese. I never throw out stale cheese but toss it into the blender or my new food processor.

3 cups mashed potatoes	1/4 tsp. pepper
1/2 cup whipping cream	1/2 tsp. salt

1/2 cup grated cheese (Parmesan is good)

Place potatoes in a casserole. (They should be mashed until very fluffy without adding butter or milk.)

Whip cream, add pepper and salt and fold in cheese.

Spread over potatoes and bake in a 350-degree oven for about 30 minutes or until top is browned. (Serves 4 to 6.)

Cutting a thin slice from each end of a potato and pricking remaining skin with a fork makes it bake 25 per cent faster.

POMMES DE TERRE FONDANTES

6 potatoes   4 tbsp. butter

Select potatoes that are of equal size and peel them.
Melt butter in a heavy frying pan and roll potatoes in it.
Cover and cook over low heat for 20 minutes. Uncover
and cook another 30 minutes, still on low heat, turning 5 or
6 times during cooking period. (They are cooked when soft
and golden brown all over.)
Serve immediately.

LYONNAISE POTATOES

1/3 cup salad oil OR melted lard   Dash of nutmeg
1 cup onion, chopped finely   Rind of half a lemon, grated
1 clove garlic, minced   1 tsp. lemon juice
6 to 8 potatoes, cut into quarters   1 tbsp. minced fresh OR dried
1 tsp. salt   parsley
Dash of pepper

Heat oil or lard in heavy pan, and fry onions and garlic
lightly.
Add potatoes and stir.
Add salt, pepper, nutmeg and grated lemon rind.
Cook over low heat for 30 minutes, covered, or till
potatoes are tender. Add lemon juice and stir. If potatoes
are too moist, cook uncovered for a few minutes.
Sprinkle parsley over top and serve. (Serves 4 to 6.)

MONIQUE'S DUCHESSE POTATOES

*This recipe came from Madame Jehane Benoit's daughter,
Monique MacDonald with whom she runs a boutique selling
produce from their lamb farm at East Hill, Quebec. It is the
ideal potato casserole to make for Christmas and other holiday
meals when you don't want to be confined to the kitchen.*

Potatoes   Shallots or grated onion (optional)
1 cup sour cream (commercial)   Salt and pepper (to taste)
Buttered crumbs

Cook as many potatoes as are needed till soft. Add
sour cream and beat till creamy.

Add onion, salt and pepper to taste and spoon into
buttered casserole. Sprinkle liberally with buttered crumbs.
(Melt butter and combine with dry crumbs.)

Place in refrigerator when cool and take out half an
hour before reheating in a 350-degree oven for 15-20 minutes.

MINTED CARROTS

*Mint is perfect for carrots, and the sherry is an added touch
which you may not approve of until you've tasted it.*

1 bunch carrots	1/8 cup sherry
Salt and pepper (to taste)	1 tbsp. butter
1/4 tsp. sugar	1 tsp. mint

Wash, scrape and cut carrots lengthwise. Cook in as
little water as possible. Sprinkle with salt, pepper and
sugar.

Drain if necessary (save water for soups and gravies),
add sherry and return to low heat.

Place in serving dish, top with butter, sprinkle with
mint and toss lightly with a fork and spoon. (Serves 3 to 4.)

NUTMEG BEETS

*This is one of those recipes, almost too simple to mention,
except that it points up the use of a spice, usually associated
with desserts. Nutmeg is fine with spinach, onions, broccoli,
cauliflower, cabbage, green peas, succotash and sweet
potatoes. It's good in soups, too.*

1 can beets, diced or cut into	2 tbsp. butter
strips, OR freshly cooked beets	Dash of nutmeg

Heat beets and drain.
Toss with butter and a dash of nutmeg.

NEW BEETS AND BEET TOPS

Beet greens make better eating than spinach, I think, and I watch longingly for their first appearance every summer. This recipe is a special one which is my favourite way of doing the greens and beets.

Remove leaves from beets, wash leaves and cut with scissors into 1/2-inch pieces. Cook beets separately.

Place in a saucepan with 1/4-cup water for each 2 cups of minced beet leaves. Salt. Cover and boil 10 minutes over high heat.

Drain. Put leaves back into saucepan. Sprinkle with 1 tsp. flour, add 1 tsp. butter and 1 tbsp. milk. Stir over high heat until creamy.

Slice boiled beets over creamed leaves and serve.

ALMOND BROCCOLI

Almonds aren't confined to broccoli when it comes to using them in main-course dishes. They should be blanched, roasted and slivered before sprinkling over broccoli, asparagus, green beans or any soup.

1 pkg. frozen broccoli	3 tbsp. butter
1/4 cup almonds, finely chopped	1 tsp. lemon juice

Cook broccoli according to directions on package and drain.

Brown almonds in butter. Add lemon juice and pour over hot broccoli.

BAKED SHALLOTS

Why not cook shallots? People who can't eat them raw find baked shallots easy to digest. I like them instead of roasted onions with a roast of beef or as part of a vegetable plate.

4 bunches shallots	Juice of a lemon
Salt and pepper	About 4 tbsp. butter OR
Nutmeg	margarine (or more)

Wash and trim shallots and place neatly in a long, narrow oven dish.

Sprinkle with salt and pepper. Place butter or margarine in one piece on top. Grate nutmeg and pour lemon juice over all.

Bake in a 500-degree oven for 15 minutes. Do not over-cook and do not allow to burn. If you're not sure of your oven, lower the heat. Baste once or twice during cooking. (Serves 4.)

SPINACH ROSEMARY

This recipe is a century old and it looks as though it will be appreciated for at least another 100 years in our family. I like raw spinach in salads, soups, but I like it best cooked with rosemary.

1 lb. spinach	1 tbsp. butter
Handful of parsley	Salt
4 to 6 green onions	1/2 tsp. rosemary

Wash spinach in a bowl of cold water and lift it in and out with the hands. The sand and dirt are removed this way much better than when the spinach is washed in a colander.

Chop parsley and onions and sprinkle among spinach, add butter, salt and rosemary.

Cover and cook, shaking pot frequently over very low heat till spinach is tender.

Note: New potatoes, boiled gently and sprinkled with chopped parsley and dill, are an ideal second vegetable. (Serves 3.)

PURÉED TURNIPS

This is just one of the many ways of turning turnip haters into turnip lovers.

1 turnip (about 1 lb.)	1 egg, beaten
4 to 5 potatoes	Salt and pepper
2 tbsp. cream	1/2 tsp. dry mustard

Boil sliced turnip in salted water till tender but not too soft (about 15 minutes).

Cook potatoes in salted water in a separate pot.   Drain and mash.

Drain turnip and mash with a heavy fork and combine with potatoes.

Add cream, egg, salt, pepper and mustard and whip with an egg beater or in the electric mixer.

Butter a casserole, pour the purée into it and bake at 400 degrees for 20 minutes.   (Serves 3 to 4.)

Some vegetable combinations you may want to try: peas and summer squash; wax beans and green beans; squash and lima beans; peas and wax beans; celery and tomatoes; squash and asparagus; peas and new potatoes; spinach and tomatoes; cabbage and beets; carrots and green beans; cauliflower and corn; peas and green onions; tomatoes and cauliflower; broccoli and mushrooms.

TURNIP WITH APPLE

One of my dearest friends, who looks as though she lived on hummingbirds' wings, always surprises me with the way she digs into a bowl of turnip and apple, served with a loin of pork at our house. Pickled crab apples take the place of apple sauce with pork when I put this vegetable on the menu.

Turnip	Butter
Boiling water	Salt and pepper
	1 cup hot apple sauce

Peel turnip, removing a thick peeling and leaving no sign of green (the bitterness is between the peeling and the vegetable).

Slice into medium-sized pieces.

Place in a saucepan and pour boiling water on top. (There should be at least 3 inches of water in pan.)

Cover and boil quickly for 15 to 20 minutes. (Never let the turnips change colour, as this means they are over-cooked.) Drain well.

Mash turnip and add apple sauce, a good-sized piece of butter and salt and pepper.

Whip until light.

SOUR CREAM SUCCOTASH

This is the best succotash I've ever eaten. It bears no resemblance to the wishy-washy collection of corn and limas which are served up with not a trace of embarrassment by some professional cooks.

1 pkg. frozen lima beans	Butter
1 can corn niblets	Salt and pepper
Few tbsp. chopped shallots	1/4 cup sour cream (commercial)

Cook lima beans as directed on package. Drain and rinse with ice water to retain colour.

Heat corn niblets, add lima beans and shallots, and allow to reheat.

Add a tablespoon or two of butter, salt and pepper, and stir in sour cream. Serve immediately.

DUTCH RED CABBAGE

The Dutch like to combine potatoes with a lot of other ingredients to make them a meal in one dish. Here, potatoes combine with cabbage and bacon.

2 tart apples	3 tbsp. butter
1 medium red cabbage	Dash of nutmeg
3 tbsp. brown sugar	Salt and pepper (to taste)
2 tbsp. vinegar	1/2 lb. lean back bacon

2 cups hot mashed potatoes

Peel and slice apples. Cut cabbage fairly finely, discarding the core.

Cook cabbage and apples in small amount of water for 10 minutes, then add brown sugar and vinegar and continue cooking until tender.

Drain and add butter, nutmeg, salt and pepper.

Dice bacon, reserving 3 slices. Fry small pieces till they are crisp and add them, with fat, to cabbage mixture.

Add potatoes, which should be freshly cooked and mashed without milk or other liquid and mix well. Taste at this point. You may want to add more seasoning.

Turn into a greased casserole, top with raw bacon slices and set under oven broiler till bacon is crisp. Or fry bacon and place on top and put in 400-degree oven for 5-10 minutes. In Holland, this recipe is usually served as a complete main dish. (Serves 3.)

SWEET AND SOUR RED CABBAGE

The first time I ate red cabbage, it came to me swimming in navy blue water and tasting terrible. Then I came on this recipe which is a favourite in our house.

2 tbsp. salad oil OR dripping	2/3 cup cider vinegar
4 cups red cabbage, shredded	2 cups hot water
2 medium-sized apples, unpeeled and chopped	4 tbsp. sugar

Heat salad oil or dripping.   Add remaining ingredients.
Bring to a boil and cook over medium heat, uncovered,
until tender (about 15 minutes).
Drain and serve, topped with a piece of butter.
(Serves 4.)

HOW TO BOIL CORN

*Corn should be prepared this way and no other, on top of
the stove. It's wonderful roasted over an open fire but if it
is to be boiled, please try it this way and you won't go back
to the old method of drowning the cobs in water and
boiling them tasteless.*

12 ears of corn, unhusked	1 cup milk
2 cups boiling water	1 tsp. sugar

Place boiling water, milk and sugar in a saucepan. Don't
add salt.
Cut about 1 inch off each ear of corn. Remove the
tough outside leaves and as much silk as you can pull from
the end, but leave a layer of husks.
Place unpeeled corn in liquid mixture. Cover and boil
quickly 15 to 20 minutes.
Send to the table unpeeled, which keeps the corn nice
and warm, or peel before serving.
News of the 70's: Corn is fabulous done in the microwave oven!

HERBED GARDEN CARROTS

Carrots are taken for granted by too many cooks. Add a few herbs, cut them into strips and you'll never go back to the old trick of cutting them up any way and serving them without a whiff of herbs.

5 or 6 medium-sized carrots	1 tbsp. minced parsley
2 tbsp. butter	1/4 tsp. thyme
1/4 tsp. sugar	2 tbsp. table cream
	1/4 tsp. salt

Clean and cut carrots into long, thin strips.

Place carrots, butter, sugar, salt, minced parsley and thyme in a saucepan. Stir together until butter is melted.

Cover and cook over very low heat about 20 minutes or until carrots are tender.

Add cream.

Simmer a few minutes and serve. (Serves 3 to 4.)

BAKED LIMA BEANS

Salt pork or bacon added to almost any vegetable during the cooking is an idea worth investigating if you've never tried it. Green beans, wax beans and any green vegetable get along just fine with pork.

1/2 cup chopped salt pork or bacon	2 cups lima beans, fresh
1/2 cup onions, chopped very finely	2 cups boiling water
1 cup carrots, scraped and diced	2 tbsp. butter
	Salt and pepper (to taste)

Cook salt pork in heavy pan for 5 minutes. Add onions, and brown.

Add carrots and beans, then season to taste.

Pour into baking dish and add water. Dot with butter.

Cover and bake about an hour at 325 degrees until tender.

HERB TOMATOES

*On a hot summer day, give me a loaf of brown bread, a glass
of milk and a bowlful of herb tomatoes for a heavenly lunch.
When I am alone, I eat tomatoes by the dozen and thank
heaven I don't get hives or whatever shows itself on some after
a session of tomato eating.*

Slice tomatoes, stem down on board, and place in bowl.

Make 1/4 cup of French dressing by combining wine
vinegar and olive or salad oil in equal parts (or two oil to one
vinegar).

Add 1/2 tsp. basil (fresh, if available), 1/2 tsp. marjoram
and a little garlic if desired.

Pour on the dressing 5 minutes before serving. Sprinkle
with minced parsley.

SAVOY GRILLED TOMATOES

*This makes marvellous eating for late Sunday breakfast along
with grilled lamb chops or chipped beef and eggs. It's one
way of using up tomatoes at the height of the season.*

3 tbsp. soft butter	1 egg yolk
1 tsp. dry mustard	Tomatoes

Mix butter with dry mustard and egg yolk.

Cut tomatoes in two. Sprinkle with salt. Place on a
plate with the cut part touching the bottom of the plate and
let stand 20 minutes.

Drain tomatoes and brush each piece with a little sugar,
then spread a little of the creamed mixture on the cut side
of each.

Place in a cold frying pan, taking care to place the
buttered side of the tomatoes down. Cook over low heat
20 minutes without turning.

Remove carefully with a spatula. Tomatoes cooked in
this way are covered with a golden paste and are most
delicious.

ZUCCHINI CRÊPES

*What a discovery some recipes are!   These are the gems you
cut out and stick onto the back pages of a recipe book.
This is one which I want to put in a permanent place.*

3 cups grated zucchini, coarse or fine   1/2 cup flour
1 egg   1 tsp. baking powder
Salt and pepper to taste   Melted butter
                    Grated Parmesan cheese

Combine grated zucchini, egg, salt and pepper in a bowl.
Sift flour and baking powder over zucchini and mix
thoroughly.
Drop by large spoonfuls onto a lightly-oiled frying pan
or griddle and cook till brown on both sides.
Serve with melted butter and grated Parmesan cheese.
These make delicious hors d'oeuvres in which case you
should make them very small.   Serves 6.

RATATOUILLE

*This delicious south-of-France vegetable stew can be eaten
hot or cold, as a main course combined with lamb or beef,
or frozen for months till needed.   Make quantities of it when
zucchini and eggplant are found at the market.*

1 eggplant   2 cloves of garlic, crushed
2-3 small zucchini   Salt and pepper
1 tsp. salt   5-7 tomatoes, peeled, seeded
4 tbsp. olive or corn oil   3 tbsp. minced parsley
1 1/2 cup sliced onions   Basil, oregano or marjoram
1 cup sliced green peppers

Chop eggplant and zucchini fairly coarsely and sprinkle
with salt.   Let stand 30 minutes in a colander to drain.
Heat oil in frying pan and sauté eggplant and zucchini
till golden.   Remove to warm dish.   Add more oil if necessary
and cook onions and peppers slowly till soft.   Stir in garlic
and season to taste with salt and pepper.
Return eggplant and zucchini to pan and stir with wooden
spoon.

Chop tomatoes into fairly large pieces and add with herbs (using any or all of the herbs) in quantities to taste.

Cook till eggplant is tender, stirring occasionally. Cook, uncovered, till much of the liquid has been evaporated. Taste for seasoning. Serves 6-8.

CASSEROLE OF ONIONS

This is an old-timer, and I like it for the wonderful aroma it creates in my kitchen. I like this casserole with boiled beef and cabbage.

2 lb. onions, sliced 1/4-inch thick	1 tsp. celery seed
1 tsp. salt	1/4 tsp. basil OR sage
1/4 tsp. pepper	3 tbsp. butter OR bacon fat
1 tsp. paprika	1/4 cup hot water

1/2 cup bread crumbs

Mix salt, pepper, paprika, celery seed and basil or sage together.

Place layers of the sliced onions in a shallow greased casserole and sprinkle the mixed seasoning between the layers.

Dot top of casserole with butter or bacon fat and pour hot water over mixture. Cover.

Bake in a 400-degree oven for 1 hour. Then sprinkle top with bread crumbs and a little melted butter to taste.

Bake, uncovered, for 15 minutes longer or until the crust is golden brown. (Serves 4 to 5.)

BASCONNAISE

This dish is well known in France. It's marvellous eating on a hot summer day, with slices of buttered bread. I have served it to friends on slimming diets, and often prepare a single portion for myself when I am at home alone.

3 raw parsnips, shredded

2 tomatoes, sliced

6 stalks celery, cut in strips

6 raw carrots, shredded

4 cups cabbage, shredded

2 cups raw turnips, shredded

1 bunch parsley

6-12 black or green olives

1 green pepper, cut into thin strips

Combine each shredded vegetable with the type of dressing you prefer. (I prefer French dressing.)

Sprinkle tomatoes with dressing and arrange all the vegetables in an attractive design on a large platter.

Garnish with olives, parsley, celery and green pepper. (Serves 4 to 6.)

EASY HOLLANDAISE SAUCE

1/4 cup cold butter

Juice of 1/2 or 1 lemon

2 egg yolks

Place ingredients in a small saucepan. It is important to start this sauce in a cold saucepan with the ingredients just out of the refrigerator.

Cook over low heat until creamy, stirring all the time, and at no time allowing the saucepan to get very hot. When saucepan starts to get hot, remove from heat and keep on stirring. Three to 5 minutes are required to cook the hollandaise. (Makes enough to serve with 2 pounds of broccoli or asparagus.)

Potato or carrot balls (made by using a melon ball cutter on the uncooked vegetable) take as long as a whole potato to cook.

Part 3

Endings

Bread, Cake, Fruit Pies

When I wrote about baking twenty years ago, I talked about it as a joyful experience. Nowadays, people are baking because it is good nutrition — and they find it is still good for the soul. I have customers, many of them young men, who come in to buy bread pans and end up giving detailed descriptions of the breads they are going home to bake — molasses, oatmeal, onion, cracked wheat — and when l empty my pocket at the end of the day, I find it full of scribbled notes of recipes and cooking ideas exchanged with other bread makers. I still find bread making the most satisfying of all baking jobs. Everyone loves to walk into a house which smells of old-fashioned bread in the oven. Kneading dough is good for tension, depression and nerves. Don't kick the cat on a bad day — make bread.

When it comes to cake, it's important to remember that the trickiest ingredient is the flour. Variations in the weight and blend of flour make a recipe behave   differently. That's why, even to this day, people get attached to one brand of flour and stay with it. If the recipe calls for pastry (or soft wheat) flour, use that or use all-purpose flour minus two tablespoons for every cup called for in the recipe.

WATER BREAD

1/2 cup lukewarm water	3 cups water
1 tsp. granulated sugar	1 tbsp. salt
1 envelope dry yeast	2 tbsp. granulated sugar
11 cups all-purpose flour, sifted	1/4 cup shortening OR margarine

Dissolve 1 tsp. granulated sugar in 1/2 cup lukewarm water. Sprinkle yeast on top of water. Let stand 10 minutes; stir well.

Place 3 cups water, salt, 2 tbsp. granulated sugar and shortening or margarine in a saucepan, and bring to a boil. Cool to lukewarm.

Place flour in a large bowl. Add well-stirred yeast and 1 cup of the lukewarm water mixture to sifted all-purpose flour, pouring it in at one side of the bowl and all in one spot.

Work it into the flour with your hands, adding the remainder of the lukewarm mixture gradually until it has all been used. When flour and liquid are well blended, put on a floured board.

Knead dough until smooth and elastic (about 10 minutes).

Place in a greased bowl and cover with a clean towel. Let rise in a warm place free from drafts for about 2 hours or until double in bulk.

Punch dough down and pull sides into the centre. Turn onto a floured board and knead for about 3 minutes.

Divide dough into three equal portions and knead each portion into a ball.

Cover with a clean towel and let stand for 10 or 15 minutes.

Place one portion of dough in round cake pan. Shape another portion of dough into a loaf and place in greased bread pan. With two thirds of the remaining portion of dough make a braid and place on greased 17 x 11-inch baking pan. Top with a small braid made from the remaining dough.

Cover all the dough with a clean towel and let rise in a warm place free from drafts for about 1 hour or until double in bulk.

Using a sharp knife, make two diagonal gashes about 2 to 2 1/2 inches apart on round loaf.

Bake in a 450-degree oven for 15 minutes, then lower heat to 350 degrees and bake 30 minutes longer.

Unmould and cool on wire cake rack. (Makes one 8-inch round loaf plus one 8 1/2 x 4 1/2 x 2 1/2-inch bread loaf plus one 13-inch long braid OR one 8 x 4-inch loaf.)

SAVORY BISCUITS

(Serve as the base for creamed chicken)

Use a biscuit mix and add 1/2 tsp. of savory or sage.

Bake biscuits according to directions, split and top with creamed chicken.

Note: Make curry biscuits by adding a teaspoon of curry powder to the dry ingredients.

BACON CORN BREAD

(Serve for breakfast or for a light supper)

1 cup flour	7/8 cup milk
4 tsp. baking powder	2 tbsp. melted shortening
1/2 tsp. salt	OR bacon fat
4 tbsp. brown sugar	1/2 cup corn kernels
1 cup corn meal	6 bacon slices
1 egg	

Preheat oven to 400 degrees.

Line an 8 x 8 x 2-inch pan with bacon slices.

Sift flour, baking powder, salt and brown sugar.

Add corn meal and stir to blend.

Beat egg, add milk, melted fat and corn kernels and stir to blend.

Pour liquid ingredients over dry ingredients and stir just enough to blend.

Pour batter into pan over bacon slices.

Bake in preheated oven from 25 to 30 minutes or till light brown on top.

To serve, unmould same as an upside-down cake. Serve hot.

ONION-CHEESE BREAD

1/2 cup onion, chopped	1 1/2 cups biscuit mix
1 tbsp. fat	1 cup grated cheese
1 egg, beaten	1 tbsp. poppy OR sesame seeds
1/2 cup milk	2 tbsp. melted butter

Cook onions in fat until tender and light brown.

Combine egg and milk and add to biscuit mix.

Stir until dry ingredients are just moistened.

Add onions and 1/2 cup grated cheese.

Spread dough in a greased 8 x 1 1/2-inch round baking dish.

Sprinkle top with remaining 1/2 cup of grated cheese and poppy or sesame seeds.

Drizzle melted butter on top.

Bake in a 400-degree oven for 20 to 25 minutes. Serve hot.

RYE BREAD

2 tsp. granulated sugar	2 tbsp. soft margarine OR
1 cup lukewarm water	shortening
2 envelopes active dry yeast	1/2 cup lukewarm water
1 tbsp. molasses	3 cups rye flour, sifted
2 tbsp. granulated sugar	1 1/4 cups all-purpose flour, sifted
1 tsp. salt	1 egg white, lightly beaten

Thoroughly dissolve 2 tsp. granulated sugar in 1 cup lukewarm water. Sprinkle yeast on top of water. Let stand 10 minutes, then stir well.

Combine molasses, 2 tbsp. granulated sugar, salt, margarine or shortening and 1/2 cup lukewarm water in a large bowl and mix well.

Add well-stirred yeast. Mix and add rye flour. Beat well.

Add all-purpose flour and when dough is stiff enough to be easily handled turn onto a floured board.

Knead until smooth and elastic (about 3 minutes).

Place in a greased bowl and brush top of dough with melted shortening.

Cover with a clean towel and let rise in a warm place, free from drafts, for about 2 hours or until double in bulk.

Punch dough down and turn onto floured table. Knead into a ball and let stand 10 minutes.

Shape into a smooth, long loaf.

Place on greased 17 x 11-inch baking sheet, and cut diagonal slashes in the loaf, about 1/8 inch deep, 1 1/2 inches apart.

Brush with lightly beaten egg white.

Let rise, uncovered, in a warm place free from draft for about 30 minutes or until double in bulk.

Bake in a 375-degree oven for 35 to 40 minutes. (Makes 1 loaf.)

FRENCH PANCAKES

1 cup table cream	3 tbsp. icing sugar
4 eggs, unbeaten	1/2 cup all-purpose flour, sifted
1 tsp. salt	

Put all ingredients in a mixing bowl.

Beat until smooth with a rotary or electric mixer.

Grease the surface of a frying pan with unsalted fat or butter.

Pour the batter from a ladle, pitcher or measuring cup. Swirl pan around to have as thin a pancake as possible.

Cook for about 1/2 to 1 minute on each side.

Spread the surface with strawberry jam and roll.

Sprinkle with icing sugar and serve hot. (Makes 14.)

BREAKFAST BRIOCHES

1/2 cup lukewarm water
2 tbsp. sugar
1 envelope dry yeast OR
   1 cake (1 oz.)
1 cup flour

4 cups flour
1 tsp. salt
1/2 cup butter, melted
3 eggs

Dissolve sugar in water. Pour yeast on top. Allow to stand 10 minutes.

Stir, add 1 cup flour and stir again.

Cover with cloth and let rise in warm place till double (about 1 hour).

Sift 3 cups of flour in large bowl.

Make a well in the centre and drop in 1 tsp. salt.

Add melted butter to well and, with a wooden spoon, stir, gradually work in flour and yeast mixture (called sponge). (If batter gets too hard, use hands instead of spoon.)

When mixed, add 1 unbeaten egg at a time and keep on kneading with hands till smooth. (Batter will be softer than bread dough, so you may find this helpful: Line the bowl with a clean cloth and sprinkle lightly with flour. Pour dough back into cloth. Fold corners of cloth to cover the dough completely.)

Let rise in warm place to double (about 1 to 2 hours, depending on the heat in the room).

Knead again in cloth when dough has risen.

Allow to rise again (30 to 45 minutes).

Knead again.

Cut off pieces of dough to form balls (or grease a muffin tin and place a ball of dough to half-fill each muffin space).

Dig out a little hole on top of the brioche (or cut a criss-cross on the top) and place another tiny ball of dough to make the crown on the brioche.

Cover and allow to double in bulk (about 25 to 40 minutes).

Brush lightly with beaten egg.

Bake in preheated oven (400 degrees) for 15 minutes. Lower to 325 degrees and bake an additional 15 minutes.

DANISH NUT CAKE

2/3 cup butter OR shortening	1 cup pastry flour
2/3 cup fine granulated sugar	1/2 tsp. baking powder
3 eggs, unbeaten	1/4 tsp. salt
1 tsp. vanilla OR 3 cardamom	1/4 to 1/2 cup walnuts, minced
seeds, crushed OR 1/2 tsp.	3 to 4 fresh rose geranium
ground cardamom	leaves (optional)

Cream butter or shortening until light and fluffy.

Add sugar, a tablespoon at a time, beating well after each addition.

Add eggs, one at a time, beating well after each addition.

Add vanilla or cardamom seeds or ground cardamom.

Sift together twice flour, baking powder and salt.

Add flour mixture by the teaspoon to creamed mixture, beating well after each addition. Fold in walnuts. (This cake requires no liquid other than eggs.)

Pour into well-greased 10 x 3 1/2 x 2 1/2-inch loaf pan. If you have them place fresh rose geranium leaves on top of cake batter before baking in a 350-degree oven for 45 to 50 minutes.

Turn out on wire rack and allow to cool for 30 minutes, top side up.

MRS. MACLEOD'S OATCAKES

This recipe came my way while we were staying at Ingonish, Nova Scotia, at Macleod's On-the-Point. We ate oatcakes instead of bread and packed them into our lunch box for the return trip to the mainland.

3 cups rolled oats	1 tsp. soda
3 cups white flour	1 1/2 cups lard
1 cup white sugar	3/4 cup cold water
2 tsp. salt	

Combine rolled oats, flour, sugar, salt and soda. Work in lard as if for pastry.

Moisten with water. Roll thin, using rolled oats on board.

Cut into squares or circles and bake in a moderate oven for about 15 minutes. Eat instead of bread.

DATE NUT LOAF

4 cups dates, cut up	1 1/2 cups brown sugar, firmly
2 cups boiling water	packed
4 cups pastry flour	2 eggs
1 tsp. salt	2 tsp. soda
1/2 cup shortening	2 cups nut meats, broken

Pour boiling water over dates. Sift pastry flour with salt.

Cream shortening and brown sugar together until light and fluffy. Add eggs and beat thoroughly.

Add soda to date mixture, then add the date mixture and the flour to the creamed mixture. Stir in broken nut meats last.

Pour into well-greased and floured bread pans or four small loaf pans.

Bake in a 350-degree oven for 45 minutes to one hour, depending on size.

Remove from pan immediately after baking. Cool on cake rack.

NEVER-FAIL CREAM PUFFS

1/2 cup water	1/2 cup all-purpose flour, sifted
1/4 tsp. salt	2 eggs
1/4 cup butter	

Boil water. Add salt and butter and bring to a boil.
Add flour all at once and stir vigorously until mixture
forms a stiff ball. Remove from heat.

Add eggs, one at a time, beating well after each
addition until mixture is smooth. (An electric mixer is good.)

Shape puffs by dropping from a tablespoon onto a
greased 17 x 11-inch baking sheet.

Bake in a preheated 425-degree oven for 15 minutes.
Reduce heat to 375 degrees and bake 25 minutes longer.
(Makes 6 large puffs.)

Split and fill with sweetened whipped cream.

CHOCOLATE COCONUT CRUST

1 1/2 cups chocolate wafer crumbs	1/4 cup melted butter
1/2 cup coconut	

Combine and press into pie pan and bake at 375 degrees
for 5 to 8 minutes.

Cool, fill with ice cream or any favourite filling.

EASY PASTRY

This recipe, from friend Doyle Klyn, is one which defies all the rules of good pastry making. As Madame Jehane Benoit said, when she chose it along with several recipes from We Can Cook, Too — *a collection published by the Montreal branch of the Canadian Women's Press Club* — *to demonstrate on television, "It shouldn't work but it does." It's the recipe for the person who has never succeeded with pastry.*

1/2 lb. shortening	1 tsp. salt
1/4 cup butter	1/4 cup cold water
3 cups all-purpose flour	

Cream shortening and butter thoroughly.

Add sifted flour and salt gradually, creaming well.

Add water and mix thoroughly. Mixture will be sticky at first and will take considerable stirring.

When rolling out this pastry use plenty of flour on the board. It will never be tough and it will keep in refrigerator for 10 days at least. Before using refrigerated pastry allow it to stand at room temperature to soften.

DOYLE'S LEMON TARTS

1 1/2 tbsp. butter	2 eggs, well beaten
3/4 cup sugar	1 tsp. mint, chopped
Rind and juice of 1 large lemon	Pastry for unbaked tart shells

Cream butter and sugar.

Add lemon juice and rind and mix well. Add eggs and, lastly, mint.

Mix well and fill unbaked tart shells (use recipe for Easy Pastry).

Bake in a 375-to-400-degree oven for about 15 minutes, or until filling has set and both it and pastry are browned. (Makes filling for 18 medium-sized tarts.)

DELICIOUS BUTTER TARTS

1 1/2 cups currants OR rasins
4 tbsp. butter (or more)
2 eggs
2 cups brown sugar

Few tsp. rum or rum flavouring
Chopped nuts
Pie Pastry

Soak currants or raisins in boiling water for a few minutes till they are plump.

Beat butter till creamy. Add eggs and brown sugar and beat until foamy.

Add rum or rum flavouring, chopped nuts and currants or raisins.

Pour filling into uncooked tart shells. (Use Easy Pastry.) Use small tart pans, as they make a daintier dessert.

Bake in a 375-degree oven for 15 to 20 minutes (or till brown). Cool slightly before removing gently from pans to a wire rack. These are much more delicious the second day, so make them in advance.

Serve with whipped cream.

PERFECT BROWNIES

2 1-oz. squares unsweetened
    chocolate
1/2 cup butter OR margarine
1 cup sugar
2 eggs

1 tsp. vanilla
1/2 cup all-purpose flour, sifted
1/2 cup walnuts, chopped

Melt chocolate in the top of a double boiler over hot water.

Cream butter or margarine and sugar thoroughly. Add eggs and beat well.

Blend in melted chocolate, vanilla and flour.

Mix nuts into batter or sprinkle them over the top after batter is poured into the pan.

Pour batter into a greased 8 x 8 x 2-inch pan.

Bake in a 325-degree oven for 35 minutes.

Frost with fudge frosting if desired. (Makes 12 large brownies.)

DOUGHNUTS

4 cups flour (approx.)	2 eggs
2 tsp. baking soda	1 1/2 cups sugar
1 tsp. cream of tartar	1 1/4 cups sour milk OR
2 tsp. salt	buttermilk
2 tsp. nutmeg	1 tbsp. melted butter

Mix and sift flour, baking soda, cream of tartar, salt and nutmeg.

Beat eggs until thick and pale in colour. Gradually beat in sugar, and then stir in the milk or buttermilk mixed with melted butter. Gradually stir in flour mixture, blending until almost smooth.

Turn out on a floured board and roll out 1/4-inch thick.

Cut with a floured cutter and fry in hot deep fat until golden (360 to 370 degrees). Drain on absorbent paper.

Note: The success of a doughnut is:

1) To use as little flour as possible. Even with the recipe stating 4 cups, you may find that you will do with 3 1/4 to 3 1/2 cups, depending on the blend of flour you use. Make the dough as light as possible and keep it under refrigeration for 1 or 2 hours, which will make the rolling much easier. Also use flour sparingly on board when cutting doughnuts.

2) The temperature of the fat is very important. Olive or vegetable oil is the best type of fat to use. Next to that are shortenings. I highly recommend the purchasing of a thermometer.

MY BEST PECAN PIE

1 uncooked pie crust
3 eggs slightly beaten
1/2 cup brown sugar OR white
    sugar
1/4 tsp. salt
1 cup light corn syrup

1/2 tsp. vanilla
1 cup pecans, broken into pieces (or
    combine pecans and walnuts)
1/2 cup heavy cream
Whole pecans for garnish

Make a rich 9-inch pie crust and refrigerate till well chilled.

Mix eggs, sugar, salt, syrup, vanilla and nuts and pour into chilled pie crust.

Bake in a 450-degree oven for 10 minutes, then reduce heat to 350 degrees and bake 35 minutes longer. Chill.

Serve with whipped cream and garnish with pecans. Serve small portions, as this pie is very rich and filling. (Serves 8 to 10.)

MOCHA MARBLE CREAM PIE

1 baked pie shell
2 cups milk
1/2 cup flour
3/4 cup sugar
1/8 tsp. salt

1 cup milk
2 eggs, well beaten
1 tsp. vanilla
2 tbsp. extra-strong black coffee
2 oz. melted chocolate

Bake pie shell and set aside to cool.

Scald 2 cups milk.

Blend flour, sugar and salt with 1 cup of milk, and pour gradually into hot milk. Stir frequently.

Cook over hot water for 20 minutes. Stir and cook over low heat until thick.

Beat eggs well and beat into hot mixture slowly. Return to low heat and cook for two minutes. Add vanilla and cool.

Divide filling into three parts.

Add extra strong black coffee to the first part and stir until thoroughly blended. Pour into baked pie shell.

Add vanilla cream mixture when partly cool.

Before mixture is completely cool, spread the third part of the filling, blended with melted chocolate, over the top.

Chill the whole pie thoroughly before serving.

FAVOURITE CHOCOLATE PIE

1 baked 9-inch pie shell	1/2 cup cold milk
4 squares unsweetened chocolate	6 egg yolks
2 cups milk	1 1/2 tsp. vanilla
1 1/4 cups sugar	6 egg whites
2 tbsp. butter	Pinch of salt
1/2 tsp. salt	3/4 cup sugar
5 tbsp. cornstarch	

Melt chocolate over hot water.   Scald 2 cups milk, add
1 1/4 cups sugar, butter, salt and cornstarch which has been
mixed with 1/2 cup cold milk.

Stir over direct heat till thickened and smooth but don't
leave it for a second or it will scorch.   Place over rapidly
boiling water and cook for 10 minutes or more till mixture
loses starchy taste.

Add chocolate and beat smooth.   Pour hot mixture over
egg yolks, which have been beaten just enough to blend. Return
to double boiler and beat with an egg beater while cooking for
2 minutes over hot water. A good way of testing the filling
is to pour some onto an inverted saucer.   The filling should
not run off.

Beat filling again, add vanilla and pour into pie shell.
Cool thoroughly.

Make a meringue by beating egg whites with a pinch of
salt and adding sugar, a tablespoonful at a time.   Spread over
filling, being sure filling is absolutely cool.

Bake at 425 degrees till delicately brown or bake at 350
degrees for 12 to 15 minutes, watching carefully in both cases
that meringue does not become too brown.

Serve pie cold but do not chill in the refrigerator.

HOT STRAWBERRY PIE

This is one of my favourite strawberry pies. The topping is light and delicious and is a happy change from the usual pie crust.

1 unbaked crust	1/2 cup sugar
1 quart strawberries	1/2 cup flour
3 eggs, separated	Whipped cream

Line a pie plate with rich pastry and fill with strawberries. Beat egg yolks well, add sugar slowly and beat until fluffy. Add flour and continue beating.

Fold in beaten egg whites last, and pour over berries.

Bake in a hot oven (375 degrees) for 8 minutes. Reduce heat to 325 degrees and bake slowly until pastry is done.

Serve hot with whipped cream.

GRAPE PIE

1 qt. stemmed Concord grapes	1 tbsp. lemon juice
3 tbsp. flour OR 2 tbsp. minute tapioca	Pastry for 2-crust pie
1 cup sugar	1 to 2 tbsp. butter

Wash, drain and pulp grapes. Chop skins finely and put aside. Heat pulp in saucepan till seeds separate. Rub through a sieve to remove seeds, and add it to grape skins.

Stir flour or tapioca and sugar together and add to grape mixture, blending well. Add lemon juice. Do not add water, as grapes provide plenty of juice.

Pour into unbaked pastry shell, dot with butter and cover with a top crust or a latticework of pastry strips. Prick the top of the crust with a fork or a sharp knife.

Moisten edge of pastry with cold water and press edges together.

Bake about half an hour at 400 degrees till top is golden brown.

Cool before serving. This pie is delicious with cheese.

DANISH PASTRY

A very popular recipe, it is easy to follow, in spite of the many steps.

4 tsp. sugar
1 cup lukewarm water
4 envelopes active dry yeast
    OR 4 pkgs. compressed yeast
1 cup milk
6 tbsp. butter OR margarine
1/2 cup sugar
2 whole eggs
1 egg yolk
1/2 tsp. salt

1/2 tsp. vanilla
1/2 tsp. lemon extract
7 cups all-purpose flour, sifted
1 1/2 cups butter OR margarine
1 egg white
1 tbsp. cold water
1 pkg. instant vanilla pudding
Jams, nuts and cherries
1/2 cup corn syrup

Dissolve thoroughly 4 tsp. sugar in the lukewarm water. Sprinkle or crumble yeast on top of water. Let stand 10 minutes.

Stir well and add milk, which has been scalded and cooled to lukewarm.

Cream together thoroughly butter or margarine and 1/2 cup sugar.

Beat 2 eggs and 1 egg yolk until light. Add salt, vanilla and lemon extract. Add to creamed mixture and beat well.

Add 3 cups of the flour to well-stirred yeast and beat until smooth. Then add egg mixture and beat well.

Gradually add remaining 4 cups flour, or just enough to make a moderately stiff dough. Turn onto a floured table or counter top and knead lightly.

Place in a greased bowl, cover lightly with a clean cloth and let rise in a warm place free from draught until it is 4 times the original bulk (about 1/2 hour or more). Punch down and knead for 1 minute.

Roll out on floured board into oblong 1/2 inch thick. Divide half the butter or margarine into small pieces, and scatter over one third of the dough.

Fold one side over to cover butter or margarine; divide remaining butter or margarine into pieces and scatter on top, then fold over remaining third of dough to cover layer of butter or margarine completely. Press down edges well.

Turn dough one-quarter way around and roll out to oblong 1/2 inch thick. Fold one quarter of the dough at each end into centre, then fold side edges to centre in same manner. Chill in the refrigerator about 1 hour.

Roll out to 1/2 inch thick, fold in fourths again and chill 1/2 hour. Roll out to oblong 1/2 inch thick once again. Dough is now ready to shape. Shape as desired.

To make pinwheels, cut strips about 1/2 inch wide and 4 inches long. Using palms of hands, roll strips to about 8 inches in length. On a flat surface, hold one end of a strip and wrap remainder of strip around it, curlicue or serpentine fashion, to form a circle. Pinch end to outer edge of dough securely. Place on greased baking sheet, cover and let rise.

To make crescents, roll out dough in large circle. Cut into wedge-shaped pieces. Beginning with the broad end of each piece, roll up tightly. Place on well-greased baking sheet and shape into crescents. After shaping dough, cover and allow to rise in a warm place free from draft for about 3/4 hour or until double in bulk. Brush with egg white mixed with cold water. Decorate with cherries, nuts, raisins, using jam or instant vanilla pudding in creases of pastry. Make the crescents or pinwheels quite small, as they rise and are prettier when small. Bake in a 450-degree-to-500-degree oven until very light brown (about 5 minutes). Reduce heat to 400 degrees and bake until done (about 15 to 25 minutes depending upon size). Brush with melted corn syrup while still hot to give them a professional glaze. These freeze beautifully. (Makes 2 to 4 dozen.)

Note: Recipe may be divided in half, but you must use one egg yolk and white as called for.

CHEESE PASTRY

1 1/2 cups pastry flour, sifted	3/4 cup shredded Canadian Cheddar
1/2 tsp. baking powder	cheese
1/4 tsp. salt	2 to 4 tbsp. cold water
1/3 cup shortening	

Sift flour, baking powder and salt. Cut in shortening until the mixture resembles coarse cornmeal.

Add cheese and mix thoroughly.

Sprinkle water over the mixture, working it in lightly with a fork until all particles are moistened. Press into a ball.

Divide pastry in half for top and bottom crust of pie, and finish in the usual manner.

BABKA

This cake-like bread is associated with Easter in many European countries. It has a number of names and variations but this is a recipe which has been tested many times and is sure-fire.

3 tsp. sugar	3 eggs, unbeaten
1/2 cup warm milk	1/2 tsp. salt
2 pkgs. active dry yeast	2 cups sifted flour
1/2 cup sifted flour	1/2 tsp. mace
1/2 cup butter OR margarine	Grated rind of 1/2 lemon
1/2 cup fruit sugar	

Dissolve 3 tsp. sugar in lukewarm milk. Add active dry yeast.

Let stand for 10 minutes.

Beat in 1/2 cup flour. (This sugar-yeast-flour mixture is called a sponge.)

Set sponge to rise free from draughts for 1 1/2 hours. (Cover top lightly with a towel.)

Beat butter or margarine until soft and add 1/2 cup fruit sugar. When very light and creamy add eggs, one at a time.

Continue beating and add salt, the sponge, sifted flour, mace and grated lemon rind. Knead until smooth and elastic. (About 1/4 cup flour may be used for kneading in addition to the above.)

Place in greased fluted tube pan 9 inches in diameter and 4 inches deep (or use a small angel food pan) and allow to rise in warm place free from draughts for about 1 hour.

Bake in 350-degree oven for 40 to 50 minutes.

Unmould on cake rack as soon as baked. When cold sprinkle with sifted icing sugar.

APRICOT CREAM PIE

Baked pie shell
1/2 lb. dried apricots
1/2 cup sugar
4 tbsp. flour
1/4 tsp. salt
3/4 cup milk

2 egg yolks
2 tbsp. butter
2 tbsp. icing sugar
1/2 tsp. vanilla extract
1 cup whipped cream
1/2 square unsweetened chocolate

Soak apricots 1/2 hour. Cook until tender, then press enough through a sieve to make 1 1/4 cups of pulp.

Mix sugar, flour and salt together. Add milk, beaten egg yolks and apricot pulp.

Cook over hot water for 20 minutes, stirring frequently.

Add butter, cool, pour into pie shell and chill.

Fold icing sugar and vanilla into whipped cream.

Spread two thirds of the cream over top of pie.

Melt chocolate over hot water, add to remaining third of the cream and swirl this onto pie.

SOUR CREAM BUTTERSCOTCH PIE

1 unbaked pie crust
1 tbsp. all-purpose flour
1 cup dark brown sugar
1/4 tsp. salt
1 cup sour cream (commercial)

2 eggs, separated
1 tsp. vanilla
1 tbsp. butter
Pinch of salt
4 tbsp. sugar

Line a pie plate with pastry and rub the top of the pastry with a little piece of soft butter. Place in the refrigerator for 30 to 40 minutes before filling. (The butter and the refrigeration prevent the bottom crust from becoming soggy.)

Mix flour, brown sugar, 1/4 tsp. salt, sour cream, slightly beaten egg yolks, vanilla and melted butter together.

Pour into prepared pie crust and bake in a 450-degree oven for 10 minutes, then reduce heat to 350 degrees and bake for 45 minutes.

Cool thoroughly and cover with a meringue prepared by mixing egg whites, pinch of salt and sugar together. Brown the meringue.

FRANCES O'BRIEN'S CHEESECAKE TORTE

3 8-oz. pkgs. cream cheese
4 egg whites
1 cup sugar
1 tsp. vanilla
2/3 cup zwieback or graham
  wafer crumbs

2 cups thick sour cream
  (commercial type)
2 tbsp. sugar
1 tsp. vanilla

Soften cream cheese with the back of a wooden spoon.

Beat egg whites until stiff in a separate bowl and add 1 cup sugar gradually.

Combine egg-white mixture and cheese, add 1 tsp. vanilla.

Place in spring form pan (3 inches deep by 8 inches wide) which has been buttered and dusted with zwieback crumbs.

Bake in a 350-degree oven for 25 minutes.

Combine sour cream, 2 tbsp. sugar and 1 tsp. vanilla.

Spread over top of cheesecake and bake 5 minutes longer in a 475-degree oven.   Do not overbake.

Sprinkle with toasted almonds or fruit in season and chill for 2 hours.   (Serves 10.)

SNIP DOODLE

This is a New England morning bread.   It is really a coffee-cake, but it makes a fine dessert cake, too.

2/3 cup sugar
2 tbsp. shortening
1 egg
1 1/3 cups flour
Pinch of salt

2 tsp. baking powder
1 tsp. vanilla
2/3 cup milk
1/2 cup sugar
1 tsp. cinnamon

Blend 2/3 cup sugar with shortening. Stir in egg.

Sift flour, salt and baking powder together. Add vanilla to milk.

Add flour and milk alternately, in small amounts, to first mixture.

Stir well and pour into an 8-inch square cake pan which has been buttered and floured.

Mix 1/2 cup sugar and cinnamon and sprinkle over batter.

Bake in a 300-degree oven for 25 minutes or until edges are a golden brown and cake tester comes out clean. As it needs to set for half an hour before serving, allow yourself a full hour from when you start it until the meal is served. It can be made the day before and reheated before serving if you wish.

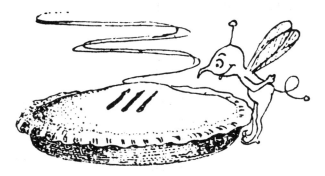

AUSTRIAN NUT TORTE

This is a delectable and very rich dessert which should be served in slim wedges. I have served it to Austrians who say it is one of the best they've tasted in Canada.

	FILLING:
1/2 cup butter	3 tbsp. butter
1 cup flour	1 1/4 cups sugar
1/2 tsp. salt	6 eggs, separated
1/4 apricot OR plum jam	1/2 lb. grated nuts (any type)

Cut butter into flour and salt and mix until very crumbly.

Pat into a 10-inch pan, covering bottom and 1/4 inch on the sides.

Bake in a 350-degree oven for 15 minutes or until light brown.

Remove from oven. Spread with jam and cover with the following mixture:

Cream butter and sugar well.

Beat egg yolks until light. Add to butter mixture and stir until well blended and foamy.

Add grated nuts gradually to the mixture, stirring well after each addition.

Beat egg whites until stiff. Carefully and gently fold into the nut mixture.

Do not handle more than absolutely necessary, as cake must remain exceedingly light.

Bake in a 325-degree oven for 30 to 40 minutes or until golden brown and firm.

PERFECT BUTTER CAKE

2 cups pastry flour	3 eggs
1/4 tsp. salt	3/4 cup milk
9 tbsp. butter or butter and shortening	1 tsp. vanilla
1 cup finely granulated sugar	2 1/2 tsp. baking powder

Preheat oven to 375 degrees.

Prepare 2 9-inch round layer pans with greased paper.

Sift, then measure, flour.

Cream butter till soft and gradually blend in sugar.

Beat eggs till thick and add to creamed mixture, a little at a time, beating well after each addition.

Measure milk and add vanilla.

Sift flour, baking powder and salt into creamed mixture, alternating with additions of the flavoured milk (make 3 dry and 2 liquid additions and combine lightly after each).

Turn batter into layer pans and spread evenly. Drop pans on table 2 to 3 times to expel large air bubbles.

Bake about 30 minutes in moderately hot oven.

Allow to stand on wire cake rack for 10 minutes, then remove from pans to cake rack and peel off paper.

EASY TWO-EGG CAKE

2 cups all-purpose flour	1/2 cup shortening
4 tsp. baking powder	1/2 cup milk
1 tsp. salt	1/3 cup lemon OR orange juice
1 1/3 cups sugar	2 eggs, unbeaten
1 tbsp. grated lemon OR orange rind	1/2 tsp. vanilla

Sift together flour, baking powder, salt and sugar.

Add to flour mixture, in the following order: grated lemon or orange rind, shortening, milk, lemon or orange juice.

Beat together for 2 minutes or until batter is well blended.

Add eggs and vanilla and beat again for 2 minutes.

Pour batter into 2 well-greased and floured 8-inch layer pans, about 1 1/4 inches deep.

Bake in a 350-degree oven for 30 to 35 minutes or until done.

Cool and frost with Lemon Fluff. (Recipe follows.)

To keep cake fresh once it is cut, place a small glass of water in the cake tin and cover. Cake keeps moist for days.

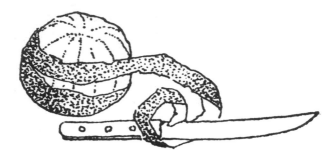

LEMON FLUFF

1 cup sugar
5 tbsp. pastry flour
1 egg, beaten
1/3 cup lemon juice

2/3 cup cold water
2 tsp. butter
1 tsp. grated lemon rind
1 cup heavy cream

Cook sugar, pastry flour, egg, lemon juice, cold water and butter together in the top of a double boiler. When thick and creamy remove from heat and cool.

Add grated lemon rind and 1/4 cup heavy cream whipped until thick. Use half of this mixture to put between the layers. Add 3/4 cup of heavy cream to the other half and whip until thick. Use as a sauce.

FRUIT CONFECTION

1/3 cup soft butter
3 tbsp. brown sugar
3 tbsp. honey
2 eggs, unbeaten
1/2 cup flour
1/2 tsp. salt
1/2 tsp. baking powder
1/8 tsp. nutmeg
1/8 tsp. allspice

1 cup candied cherries (left whole)
3/4 cup diced candied orange peel
1/2 cup diced candied lemon peel
1/4 cup diced candied mixed peel
2 1/2 cups pecan halves
Hot corn syrup
2 slices preserved pineapple
2 tbsp. orange juice

Cream butter, add sugar and beat until creamy. Add honey and eggs and beat about 4 minutes or until light and fluffy.

Sift together flour, salt, baking powder, nutmeg and allspice. Add to creamed mixture, alternating with orange juice.

Spread one third of batter over bottom of 8-inch layer cake pan that has been well buttered.

Add fruit, peel and pecans to remainder of batter, reserving a few cherries and pecans for the top.

Pile mixture on top of batter in pan, packing down and levelling the top. Decorate with preserved pineapple, cherries and nuts.

Cover with brown paper, tie securely and set in shallow pan containing hot water.

Bake for one hour at 300 degrees. Remove pan from water and bake another hour. When done, brush top with hot corn syrup and cool completely in pan set on wire rack. Cut into serving pieces.

POPOVERS THAT POP

I know that recipes for popovers can be found in practically any cookbook so I may not, on the surface, be offering anything new. The difference with these is that they do POP!

2 eggs	1 cup all-purpose flour, sifted
1 cup milk	1/2 tsp. salt

Break eggs into a bowl and add milk, flour and salt.

Mix together with a spoon, just enough to blend in the eggs.

Disregard any lumps and fill 6 well-greased custard cups three-quarters full. Set them in muffin tins for easy handling.

Place in a cold oven and start heat at 450 degrees. Do not open your oven for half an hour.

Remove from oven and make slits on 4 sides of top to let out steam and serve immediately. If you wish to reheat popovers, place in a 350-degree oven for 5 minutes. (Makes 6.)

MOCHA TORTE

Half a pound of butter in the filling may discourage some cooks who aren't used to using butter as freely as do the French. This is a lovely recipe for a party and I would advise you to throw caution to the winds and invest in half a pound of butter for this dessert.

1 sponge cake	4 tbsp. icing sugar
Mocha filling	1 tsp. vanilla
1/2 pint whipping cream	1/2 cup chopped cherries

Slice cake into 4 to 6 layers, using a long, thin knife.

Fill each layer, except top one, with mocha filling (recipe is given below) and let stand overnight in the refrigerator.

To serve, whip cream, sweeten with icing sugar and vanilla, and fold in cherries, or use them as a garnish.

Cover cake, sides and top, with whipped cream and chill in refrigerator till ready to serve.

Slice into thin pieces, as cake is rich.   (Serves 12.)

MOCHA FILLING

1/2 lb. butter	2 egg yolks
2 cups icing sugar	2 oz. melted unsweetened chocolate
Pinch of salt	4 tbsp. strong cold coffee
1 tsp. vanilla	2 beaten egg whites

Cream butter till very soft (use mixer if you have one).

Gradually add icing sugar, salt and vanilla.

Add egg yolks.

Beat till very smooth.

Add melted chocolate and coffee (4 tbsp. cold water mixed with 1 tbsp. instant coffee may be used).

Mix well and fold in beaten egg whites.

Chill well before using. Filling may ooze out of cake at first, but when it settles it will be fine.

SELF-ICED DATE CAKE

This is a very good recipe for the busy person to make because it keeps well in the bread box and is a good lunch-box item.

1 cup boiling water	1 egg
1 cup dates (1/4 lb.), chopped	1 1/2 cups all-purpose flour
1 tsp. soda	(sifted before measuring)
1 cup granulated sugar	1 tsp. salt
1/2 cup shortening	1 tsp. vanilla

Pour boiling water over chopped dates and soda. Let stand while mixing batter.

Cream sugar and shortening. Add egg and beat well.

Add flour, sifted with salt, and mix alternately with date-and-soda mixture.

Add vanilla.

Pour into a greased and floured 9 x 12-inch pan and bake in a 350-degree oven for 45 minutes. In the meantime, mix icing as follows:

4 tbsp. butter OR margarine,	2 tbsp. milk
melted	1 cup coconut OR chopped nuts
1/2 cup brown sugar	

Blend ingredients and spread evenly over cake. Put cake under broiler.

Broil icing until lightly browned and cool cake before serving. (This is a very moist cake that will keep well for several days. Do not remove from pan.)

CHRISTMAS CAKE

2 cups raisins
1 cup currants
1 1/2 cups seeded raisins, cut
1 1/2 cups maraschino cherries
1 cup dates, cut in quarters
1 1/2 cups mixed peel
1/2 cup candied pineapple
1 tbsp. preserved ginger, chopped
1 cup almonds, blanched and
  halved
3 cups pastry flour, sifted
1 tsp. cinnamon
1/2 tsp nutmeg
1/4 tsp. mace
1/4 tsp. cloves
3/4 tsp. salt
1 1/2 tsp. baking powder
1 cup butter
1 1/4 cups lightly packed brown
  sugar (or 1 cup finely granulated
  sugar)
6 eggs
1/4 cup molasses
1/3 cup grape juice OR sherry

Prepare fruits.

Sift together 3 times flour, spices, salt and baking powder.

Add fruits and nuts a few at a time, mixing until all are separated and coated with flour.

Cream butter gradually; blend in sugar.

Add unbeaten eggs one at a time, beating well after each addition.

Stir in molasses.

Add flour mixture to creamed mixture alternately with liquid, mixing well after each addition.

Turn batter into one 8 x 8 x 3-inch pan or 2 pans, one 6 x 6 x 2 1/2-inch and any smaller pan, and line with 2 layers of brown paper (greased).

Bake in a 300-degree oven for 2 3/4 to 3 hours.

Let stand in crock or tin two or three weeks, or wrap well in foil or cheesecloth soaked in brandy or rum.

Ice with almond paste and ornamental frosting.

LEMON NUT REFRIGERATOR COOKIES

2 cups all-purpose flour, sifted
1/4 tsp. baking soda
1/4 tsp. salt
1 cup shortening
1/2 cup brown sugar, firmly
packed

1/2 cup granulated sugar
1 egg, well beaten
2 tbsp. lemon juice
1 tbsp. lemon rind, grated
1/2 cup walnuts, chopped

Sift flour, baking soda and salt together.

Work shortening with a spoon until fluffy and creamy. Add brown and granulated sugars slowly, while continuing to work until light.

Add egg, lemon juice and rind and mix well.

Add flour mixture with nuts. Mix well.

Form into a roll, 2 inches in diameter.

Wrap in wax-paper and chill several hours or overnight in refrigerator.

Cut with a sharp, thin knife, using sawing motion, into 1/4-inch slices.

Arrange 2 inches apart on greased cookie sheets.

Bake in a 400-degree oven for 10 to 12 minutes or until done. (Makes about 4 1/2 dozen.)

FREEZER OR REFRIGERATOR COOKIES

3/8 cup shortening
1 cup brown sugar
1/2 tsp. grated lemon rind
1 egg, well beaten
1/2 cup walnuts OR pecans,
chopped

1 3/4 cups sifted all-purpose flour
1 1/2 tsp. baking powder
1/4 tsp. salt
1/2 tsp. cinnamon
1/8 tsp. cloves

Cream shortening, sugar and lemon rind together. Add eggs and nuts.

Sift the remaining dry ingredients together and add to the creamed mixture in three additions. The batter will be quite stiff and the last bit of flour can be kneaded in.

Shape into a roll 1 1/2 by 2 inches in diameter, wrap in wax-paper and chill or freeze.

Cut into thin slices, bake on oiled cookie sheets in a 375-degree oven 8 to 10 minutes. (Makes about 40 cookies.)

BEST OATMEAL COOKIES

1 cup light or dark raisins
2/3 cup shortening
1 1/2 cups sugar
2 eggs
1/2 cup milk
1 tsp. vanilla

2 cups all-purpose flour, sifted
1/2 tsp. soda
1 tsp. salt
1 tsp. baking powder
1 tsp. cinnamon
2 1/2 cups quick-cooking rolled oats

Rinse and drain raisins.

Cream shortening and sugar together thoroughly.

Stir in beaten eggs, milk, vanilla and raisins.

Sift together flour, soda, salt, baking powder and cinnamon.

Combine with oats and stir into creamed mixture, mixing thoroughly.

Drop by teaspoonfuls onto greased baking sheet.

Bake in a 350-degree oven 12 to 15 minutes. (Makes about 5 doz. cookies.)

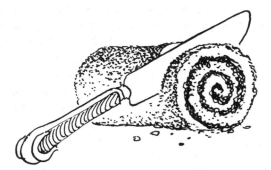

The Perfect Ending

A few svelte sophisticates may scorn desserts but I don't
think they're going to change the fact that most people like
them.   For any kind of dinner party, a good dessert is a
must, even to people who don't ordinarily eat them.   There
are two categories of desserts in my collection — those done
in a hurry and those which take time and effort.   The best
emergency dessert, of course, is fruit in season and cheese.
Frozen fruits are marvellous in fruit salads or puréed in the
blender or food processor and poured over ice cream, custard
or yogurt.   A spurt of liqueur, kirsch, brandy, grand marnier
or any flavour you favour changes fruit from a mere treat to
a triumph.   For instance, a can of black cherries becomes
spectacular when perfumed with kirsch — so do fresh pineapple and strawberries.   Though it's expensive, a bottle of
kirsch needn't be an extravagance — one lasts two years for
me since it is used only for perfuming desserts.   Then, there
are yummy, creamy, absolutely sinful creations which send
you away from the table threatening never to eat another
dessert as long as you live.   You will find some of both
groups in this chapter.

FRUIT AND CUSTARD

3 cups fruit (pineapple, pears,
    seedless grapes, peaches, berries,
    apples)
Soft custard

1/4 lb. marshmallows, quartered
    (or use whole miniature marsh-
    mallows)
2 tbsp. lemon juice

Combine fruit, add marshmallows, pour into shallow crystal or china bowl, cover with custard (see recipe below) and chill overnight.

CUSTARD

1/8 cup sugar
1/4 cup powdered milk
1/4 tsp. salt
1/4 cup fresh milk

1 whole egg OR 2 egg yolks
3/4 cup fresh milk
Few drops egg OR yellow colouring
2 tbsp. lemon juice

Combine sugar, powdered milk and salt in a metal saucepan and stir well.

Add 1/4 cup fresh milk and egg or egg yolks and beat till smooth.

Stir in 3/4 cup fresh milk and colouring and put in cooking thermometer (if you have one). Cook for about 4 minutes over medium heat, stirring constantly till cooking thermometer reaches 175 degrees or till mixture coats the spoon.

Remove from heat and chill. Flavour with lemon juice. Chill and pour over fruit. (Serves 4.)

MELBA PEACHES

1 tsp. vanilla extract
1 cup granulated sugar
1 cup water
8 fresh peaches, peeled and cut into halves

1 pint fresh raspberries
1/4 cup confectioners' sugar
2 tbsp. brandy (optional)
1 quart vanilla ice cream

Combine vanilla, sugar and water and cook until sugar dissolves.

Poach peach halves in this syrup for 8 minutes and remove from heat.

Crush raspberries. Add confectioners' sugar and brandy and mix well.

Place two peach halves in each dessert dish over a scoop of ice cream.

Top with raspberry mixture and serve. (Serves 8.)

OPEN FRUIT FLAN

PASTRY
1/4 lb. butter
2 cups flour
1/4 tsp. baking powder
1/2 tsp. salt
1 cup sugar

FILLING
12 peach OR pear halves
1 tsp. cinnamon
2 egg yolks
1 cup sour cream

Mix butter, flour, baking powder and salt plus 2 tablespoons of the measured sugar with a pastry blender.

Press dough into pie plate or quiche pan.

Arrange peaches or pears in pastry shell. Sprinkle with cinnamon and remaining sugar.

Bake for 15 minutes in a 350-degree oven.

Mix egg yolks with cream and pour over the partially baked pie. Bake 30 minutes longer and serve warm.

Note: When pears are used, a few teaspoons of chopped ginger give the dessert a sharper flavour.

Grated orange rind reduces the sweetness of whipped cream and is a delicious change.

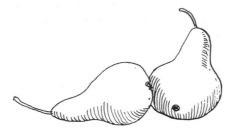

PEARS IN PORT

2 cups port wine	3 or 4 bruised cloves
1 cup sugar	6 fresh pears (ripe and ready
1/2 tsp. vanilla	to eat)

Combine all of the above ingredients except the pears.

Pare, halve and core pears and simmer in the wine syrup very gently from 45 minutes to 1 hour. When done, pears should be translucent and ruddy coloured.

Remove pears and reduce syrup until quite thick. Pour over pears.

Chill and serve with cheese tray for a perfect combination. (Serves 6.)

DESSERT IN A GLASS

1 peach half per person	1 ounce sherry or port per person

Place peach half in bottom of glass.

Pour sherry or port over it and allow to sit in the refrigerator for half an hour.

This is a spoon-and-sip dessert so any type of glass may be used. I have used large wine glasses, old-fashioned glasses and punch cups.

The peach should be pricked with a fork and eaten after the sherry has been drunk.

CHERRIES ON ICE

1 tbsp. cornstarch	1 1/2 pints vanilla ice cream
Pinch of powdered cloves	1 large meringue shell OR cream
1 large can Bing cherries	puffs (use a mix)

Combine cornstarch and cloves. Drain cherries and blend in liquid. Cook over medium heat, stirring occasionally, till it begins to thicken.

Remove from heat and stir in cherries. Sauce and meringue shell may be prepared a day ahead. At serving time arrange ice cream in spoonfuls or mounds in meringue shell or in split cream puffs, and pour on cherry sauce.

Serve immediately. (Serves 8.)

APPLES IN SYRUP

1 cup maple syrup	1 tbsp. cornstarch
1/2 cup water	1/2 cup cream
4 large apples	Pinch of salt
1 tbsp. butter	2 tbsp. brandy (optional)

Use a pot which is just wide enough to hold the apples. This helps to keep them firm.

Combine syrup and water and boil for 3 minutes while you are coring the apples.

Place apples in boiling syrup and simmer for approximately half an hour till tender. Turn them now and then so that they absorb syrup.

Place apples gently in an oven-proof dish and keep them warm in the oven.

Boil syrup until only about 1/2 cup remains.

Melt butter in another pan and add cornstarch which has been blended with the cream. Add salt, the 1/2 cup of syrup and brandy if desired, and simmer till the raw taste of cornstarch is gone.

Pour sauce over apples and serve. (Serves 4.)

APPLE CRUNCH

4 tbsp. butter	1/4 cup boiling water
1 cup brown sugar	1 tsp. vanilla
6 tart apples	1 cup flour
1 egg	1/2 tsp. baking powder
1 cup granulated sugar	Pinch of salt

Melt butter over low flame (use an oven-proof pot which can be used on top of the stove), add brown sugar and prepare apples while sugar and butter are blending.

Peel and core apples, cut them into quarters and add to butter and sugar and stir around till every piece of apple is coated.

Beat egg and granulated sugar till light, add boiling water and vanilla.

Sift flour, baking powder and salt together, then sift into egg mixture and stir to make a batter.

Pour batter on top of apples and place in a 375-degree oven till top is crusty, about 1 hour.   (Serves 4.)

OLD-FASHIONED APPLE PUDDING

2 cups beef suet, chopped	1/2 tsp. salt
1 cup unpeeled apples, chopped	1 tsp. soda
2 cups dry raisins	2 tsp. cinnamon
1 cup dry currants	1/2 tsp. cloves
1 cup molasses	1/2 tsp. allspice
1 cup apple juice OR white wine	3 eggs, beaten
3 cups flour	

Mix suet, apples, raisins, currants, molasses and apple juice or wine together.

Combine dry ingredients and add to the first mixture alternately with eggs beaten in a cool room (or better, outside in the snow).

Fill a buttered mould two-thirds full.   Cover.

Place on a rack or an inverted pie plate in a pot.   Pour 3 cups of boiling water into the pot and cover.

Cook for 3 hours over a high heat and serve with butter sauce (recipe follows).

BUTTER SAUCE

1/4 cup butter
2 tbsp. flour

2 tbsp. sugar
1 cup fruit juice

Melt butter. Add flour and sugar.
Moisten with fruit juice of your choice.
Cook just to the thickening point and flavour to taste.
(Sherry or brandy is an excellent addition.)

SWEDISH MERINGUE

1 sponge cake
1/2 cup apple sauce
3 egg whites

1/2 cup sugar
1/2 cup whipping cream

Butter a baking dish, place cake in it.
Spoon apple sauce over cake.
Beat egg whites until thick, adding sugar gradually.
Spread meringue on apple sauce and place dish in a pan of hot water.
Bake in a slow oven (about 300 degrees) until meringue is slightly brown.
Serve with whipped cream. (Serves 6.)

FRUIT WITH CREAM SAUCE

2 tbsp. butter
2 tbsp. flour
1 cup table cream
1/2 cup sugar
1/2 tsp. almond extract

1/2 tsp. vanilla extract
2 to 3 cups fresh or canned fruit, drained
Almonds, toasted and salted

Melt butter in top of double boiler, stir in flour, add cream and stir until sauce is smooth and creamy. Add sugar and stir until dissolved.
Remove from heat and add extracts.
Place fruit in centre of a crystal dish and make a border around them with sauce. Decorate with almonds. (Serves 6.)

MELON SURPRISE

1 large honeydew melon OR
  cantaloupe
Bing cherries (optional)
Peaches
Lemon juice
Frozen raspberries

Blueberries, blackberries, strawberries,
  grapes or any fruit in season
1/4 cup granulated sugar
1/2 cup kirsch OR brandy (optional)

Remove pulp from the melon with a melon ball cutter.

Remove stones from cherries, skin peaches and cut them into cubes. Sprinkle with a little lemon juice to avoid brown spots.

Mix fruit and place in a crystal bowl or a large brandy snifter.

Thaw a package of raspberries, then press through a sieve to remove seeds, flavour with sugar and liqueur and pour over fruit.

Cover and place in refrigerator for most of the day.

This is a dessert by itself or it can be used as a wonderful topping for vanilla ice cream.

FRUIT À LA SAVARIN

1 cup fresh or frozen raspberries
1/4 cup grape jelly
1/4 cup sugar
1 tsp. cornstarch

2 tbsp. lemon OR orange juice
3 to 4 cups fruit, sliced (peaches,
  pears, apples, oranges, melon, etc.)

Place raspberries, grape jelly and sugar in a saucepan. Bring to a boil and cook for 5 minutes over medium heat.

Thicken with cornstarch which has been mixed with the orange or lemon juice. Cook briefly till flavour of uncooked cornstarch is gone. Strain through a sieve.

Place prepared fruit in a serving dish. Cover with raspberry sauce and serve cold. (Serves 6.)

Bottles and pitchers which held milk or cream are much easier to wash if first rinsed in cold water.

FRESH FRUIT DIP

4 oz. cream cheese	Fresh fruit in season (whole,
1 tbsp. sugar	unhulled strawberries; unpeeled
4 tbsp. sweet cream	pear quarters; banana fingers,
1 tsp. vanilla	etc.)

Cream cheese until smooth.

Blend in sugar and gradually beat in cream and vanilla. Adjust to dipping consistency by adding more cream if necessary.

Fill a bowl with cream-cheese mixture and centre it on an attractive round platter. Arrange around it fresh fruit in season for dipping.

BAKED BANANAS

3 tbsp. butter	6 firm bananas
6 tbsp. sugar	3 tbsp. rum OR sherry
3 tbsp. lemon juice	

Melt butter. Stir in sugar and lemon juice and blend. Remove from fire.

Peel bananas and place them in a glass baking dish slightly separated from each other.

Sprinkle with rum or sherry, pour the butter sauce over and bake in a 350-degree oven for half an hour. Baste several times with the butter sauce while baking.

Serve from the baking dish. (Serves 6.)

215

STRAWBERRY CROÛTE

1 slice white bread for each
  person served

Strawberries, sliced and sweetened
1 bowl whipped or sour cream

Fry sliced bread in butter, browning one side slightly more than the other.

Place bread on a plate, browned side up, and cover with a generous quantity of sliced, sweetened strawberries.

Serve with whipped or sour cream.

STRAWBERRY SAUCE

Fresh berries in season, sliced and
  sugared OR 1 box frozen
  berries without sugar
1/2 cup canned pineapple, grated

1/2 cup pineapple juice
Handful crystallized ginger,
chopped

Combine ingredients.
Serve on ice cream.

STRAWBERRY ICE CREAM

1 1/2 cups strawberries, crushed
  OR 1 pkg. frozen
2 tbsp. lemon juice
1/4 cup sugar

1/8 tsp. salt
2/3 cup sweetened condensed milk
1/2 cup cold water
1 cup heavy cream, whipped

Add lemon juice and sugar to strawberries. If you use frozen berries thaw them out ahead of time, and you may wish to use less sugar.

Combine the remainder of the ingredients, and add the berry mixture.

Pour into freezing tray and freeze, stirring at least twice as the mixture hardens. (Serves 4 to 5.)

Making meringue? It will stand up better if half a teaspoon of baking soda is added to egg whites before they are beaten.

EASY STRAWBERRY ICE CREAM

1 qt. vanilla ice cream	2 egg yolks
1 box frozen strawberries	1/2 cup sugar
1 cup whipping cream	Red vegetable colouring (optional)
1 tsp. vanilla	

Allow ice cream to soften.
Stir in partly thawed frozen strawberries.
Whip cream until thick. Stir in vanilla.
Beat egg yolks with sugar until light.
Stir into the strawberry mixture, alternating with the whipped cream.
Add colouring to taste.
Place in freezing tray of refrigerator. Stir twice while freezing. (Add 1/4 cup of sherry, if desired.)

DEVONSHIRE STRAWBERRY

Fresh strawberries	1 tbsp. sour cream (commercial)
1 tsp. maple syrup OR brown sugar	

Fill an individual glass mould with fresh strawberries.
Sprinkle with maple syrup or brown sugar.
Top with sour cream. (This is recipe for one portion. Increase amounts as required.)

STRAWBERRY BUTTER

Summer weekend guests, I have found, expect a hostess to provide a few extra touches to her meals on their account, in spite of the promises on both sides for no fuss. This is the easiest touch I know to make a breakfast charming.

2 tbsp. butter
2 tbsp. cream cheese

4 tbsp. strawberry jam
Nutmeg OR mace

Cream butter and cheese together until light and fluffy.
Add jam (or use marmalade if desired).
Sprinkle lightly with nutmeg or mace.
Stir till well blended and creamy.
Place in a pretty jar or bowl, cover and refrigerate until ready to use on hot toast. (Sufficient to spread on 8 to 10 pieces.

RASPBERRY SAUCE

1 pkg. frozen raspberries
2 tbsp. cornstarch
1/2 cup currant jelly

2 tbsp. sugar
2 tbsp. butter
1/2 cup port wine

Thaw raspberries and drain juice into a saucepan.
Add cornstarch, jelly and sugar. Cook until thick (about 5 minutes).
Add butter and cool slightly.
Stir in wine and raspberries.
Serve warm or cold over sponge cake or pudding. (Makes about 1 1/2 cups sauce)

NORWEGIAN RASPBERRIES

1 qt. ripe red raspberries
2 tsp. water
1 cup red currant jelly
3 tbsp. cold water

1 1/2 tbsp. cornstarch
1/2 cup cream, whipped
1/2 cup almonds, slivered

Wash berries and put them through a fine sieve or in the blender. (After blending, raspberries should be put through a fine strainer to remove seeds.)

Add 2 tsp. water to seeds, bring to a boil and put through strainer again. This is to get every last drop of raspberry juice and pulp off seeds. Discard seeds.

Simmer raspberry juice and currant jelly till dissolved.

Stir 3 tbsp. water and cornstarch to a smooth paste, add to raspberry juice and cook over low heat till mixture has reached the consistency of a thin custard.

Pour it into a crystal bowl and allow it to cool, then place in refrigerator for several hours.

Cover with whipped cream and almonds and serve in your best dessert bowls. This dessert does not hold its shape, so don't think things have gone wrong if it spreads out on the plate — that's the way it's supposed to be. (Serves 4.)

FRESH CHERRY MOULD

1 1/2 lb. red ripe cherries	1 cup flour
Brandy OR fruit juice	2 cups milk
4 eggs	Sugar
1/3 tsp. salt	Whipped cream (sweetened)

Wash, dry, stem and pit cherries. Marinate them in a little brandy or any fruit juice.

Beat eggs.

Combine salt and flour, then add alternately with milk to beaten eggs. The paste should be smooth and creamy, but not thick.

Drain cherries.

Arrange them in a greased 9-inch baking dish and distribute the paste evenly over them.

Dot with butter and bake in a 325-degree oven for about 1 hour.

Sprinkle with sugar on removal from oven.

Serve with whipped cream. (Serves 4 to 6.)

Orange strips are easy to obtain for drinks and desserts if you use your vegetable peeler.

RICE SUPREME

5 cups cooked rice   Frozen fruit
1 cup whipped cream   Chopped nuts

    Combine rice with whipped cream.
Pack into a lightly oiled ring mould and chill all day.
Turn out on attractive plate.   Thaw fruit and fill hole
in centre with it.
Serve with a bowl of chopped nuts.   (Serves 8.)

CANDY CANE PARFAIT

*A delicious dessert for children.   I usually serve it on
Christmas Day.*

1 candy cane   1 cup powdered sugar
1 cup whipping cream   2 or 3 candy canes
1 qt. less 1 cup whipping cream

    Melt 1 candy cane in 1 cup whipping cream in a double
boiler.
Whip a quart less 1 cup whipping cream.   Add 1 cup
sugar as you whip.
Pour melted candy cane slowly into whipped cream
beating slowly.   Taste for sweetening.
Pour into loaf pan or refrigerator tray and freeze.
When parfait is half frozen break 2 or 3 canes into small
pieces and stir in.
Serve with chocolate sauce (recipe follows).

CHOCOLATE SAUCE

1 8-oz. pkg. semi-sweet chocolate   1/4 cup sugar
1/4 cup water   1/4 cup table cream

    Melt chocolate, water and sugar together in the top of
a double boiler over hot water.
Stir until smooth.   Remove from heat and blend in table
cream.
Serve at room temperature.

CHRISTMAS TRIFLE

Sponge cake (a day old)	Boiled custard
Sherry	Whipped cream
Brandy (optional)	Vanilla
Jam (raspberry is commonly used)	Chopped cherries and nuts

Line your prettiest crystal bowl with slices of sponge cake (lady fingers may be used in addition to sponge cake if desired).

Soak with sherry (1 cup of a good, fairly sweet sherry will do for 6 persons). For extra flavour, a small amount of brandy may be added here.

Spread with jam. Cover with boiled custard (an easy and good recipe follows) and chill well.

Cover with whipped cream which has been flavoured with vanilla at serving time, and decorate with cherries and nuts.

BOILED CUSTARD

1/4 cup sugar	2 cups fresh milk
1/2 cup powdered milk	2 whole eggs or 4 egg yolks
1/8 tsp. salt	Vanilla

Combine sugar, powdered milk and salt in a metal saucepan. Add 1/2 cup milk and eggs or egg yolks and beat till smooth.

Stir in remainder of milk and cook over moderate heat, stirring constantly about 4 minutes, or till mixture coats the spoon.

Remove from heat and chill. Flavour with vanilla.

Pour over trifle (above). This custard is also delicious served with any fresh, frozen or canned fruit.

Apples and nuts are nature's perfect dessert. Combined with a good domestic cheese, this is one dessert which is distinctly Canadian.

CHOCOLATE CHARM

1 6-oz. pkg. chocolate bits	1/2 pt. heavy cream, whipped
2 eggs, separated	1 angel food or sponge cake
1 tbsp. sugar	1/2 cup nuts, broken

Melt chocolate in top of double boiler.

Beat egg yolks until thick, then add them to melted chocolate. Mix well and cool for a few minutes.

Beat egg whites until stiff. Add sugar gradually and continue beating until sugar is dissolved.

Fold in whipped cream.

Combine cream mixture with chocolate mixture.

Remove all the outer brown crust from angel-food cake.

Break (don't cut) cake into small pieces.

Place a layer of the cake pieces in the bottom of a 7 x 12 x 9-inch pan.

Cover with half of the chocolate mixture.

Sprinkle half of the nuts on top.

Add another layer of cake, the rest of the chocolate and the remainder of the nuts.

Chill overnight in the refrigerator. (Serves 8 to 10.)

DE LUXE PLUM PUDDING

6 eggs
2 cups milk
4 cups flour
1/2 cup rum
2 cups brown sugar
1/2 cup molasses
1/2 lb. seedless raisins
1/2 lb. currants
1/2 lb. finely chopped walnuts

1 cup dates, chopped
1/2 cup mixed peel
1/4 lb. butter
1/4 lb. suet, chopped finely
1/2 tsp. nutmeg
1/4 tsp. cinnamon
1/2 tsp. salt
2 cups bread crumbs

Beat eggs.

Pour in milk slowly, stirring all the time.

Stir flour in to make a smooth cream and add rum.

Then, in order, stir in raisins, currants, walnuts, dates, mixed peel, butter, suet, nutmeg, cinnamon and salt. Mix thoroughly.

Knead in bread crumbs. (The amount of crumbs may be a little more or less than 2 cups. It must be adjusted to have the mixture fairly solid at this point.)

Steam 3 to 4 hours.

Store in a cool, dry place for as long as possible — the longer the better.

To serve, steam again 1 hour. Serve with a hard sauce.

SUPERB HARD SAUCE

1 cup sweet butter
1 1/2 cups icing sugar

1/4 tsp. nutmeg
2 tbsp. rum or brandy

Set butter to soften, but do not melt.

Cream thoroughly.

Beat in sugar a little at a time and continue to beat vigorously for 10 minutes until sauce is very smooth and creamy.

Beat in nutmeg and rum or brandy until they are completely absorbed.

Chill 12 to 24 hours.

EASTERN TOWNSHIPS PLUM PUDDING

2 cups mixed peel, diced
1 1/2 cups seedless raisins
1/2 cup sultana raisins
1 cup pitted dates, chopped
1 cup walnuts, chopped
1 cup canned crushed pineapple
   drained
2 1/2 cups all-purpose flour, sifted
1 tsp. baking powder
1 1/2 tsp. baking soda
1/2 tsp. salt

3/4 tsp. cinnamon
1/2 tsp. nutmeg
1/4 tsp. ground cloves
1/2 cup soft shortening
1/4 cup soft butter OR margarine
1 cup brown sugar, packed
4 eggs, unbeaten
1/4 cup pineapple juice
1 square unsweetened chocolate
   melted

Grease a 3-quart mould or use clean empty cans from fruit, coffee or vegetables. Two No. 2 cans and one No. 2 1/2 can or 4 No. 2 cans will take this amount.

Sprinkle the mould or cans lightly with sugar.

Combine preserved fruit, raisins, dates, walnuts and pineapple. Over these sift together flour, baking powder, soda, salt, cinnamon, nutmeg and cloves. Toss all together.

Mix shortening thoroughly with butter or margarine and sugar (if using an electric mixer, set at medium speed or cream). Then mix in eggs, pineapple juice and chocolate until mixture is very creamy (about 4 minutes altogether).

Add fruit-flour mixture gradually, combining well.

Pour into mould or cans, filling each can two-thirds full.

Cover with heavy wax-paper or foil, tie securely and place on a trivet in a deep kettle. Add enough water to come half-way up sides of mould or cans.

Cover and steam for 3 hours, No. 2 cans for 2 hours and No. 2 1/2 cans for 2 1/2 hours. Test with a straw, which should come out clean.

Remove pudding from mould or cans, cool, wrap and refrigerate till ready to serve.

CARAMEL FLOATING ISLAND

4 eggs, separated
1/2 cup sugar
1/4 cup sugar
2 1/2 cups milk

1/2 tsp. vanilla
1/2 cup sugar
2 tbsp. water

Beat egg yolks until light. Add 1/2 cup sugar and keep on beating until well mixed. Set aside.

Beat egg whites until stiff with 1/4 cup sugar.

Bring milk to a boil in a shallow saucepan or large frying pan. Add egg-white meringue to it, a large spoonful at a time. Do not cook too many spoonfuls together.

Cook each ball 1 minute, then turn with a large spatula and cook 1/2 minute on the other side. Drain with a perforated spoon and place each ball of egg white on a large platter, one next to the other.

Add milk to beaten yolks. Stir quickly over low heat until the mixture reaches the texture of a custard. Do not let it boil. Add vanilla and pour over cooked egg whites on platter.

Cook together in a heavy frying pan 1/2 cup sugar and water until syrup is golden brown. Quickly dribble it over the eggs until the top is completely coated. Serve cold. (Serves 6 to 8.)

CHOCOLATE ANGEL CAKE

1 large angel cake
2 cups whipping cream

2/3 cup chocolate sauce
1 pkg. English toffee

Cut cake into 2 layers.

Whip cream, fold in chocolate sauce and frost lower half of cake with part of the cream mixture.

Sprinkle with toffee, which has been crushed. Keep some for topping.

Place top layer neatly on bottom layer, frost top and sides with remainder of chocolate cream and sprinkle with toffee. This cake must be refrigerated at least 8 hours before serving. (Serves 16.)

CREAM CATALANE

20 macaroons, lady fingers OR
   fingers cut from sponge cake
1/4 cup fruit juice OR sherry

1/2 pt. whipping cream
1/4 cup icing sugar
Semi-sweet chocolate, shaved

Dip macaroons, lady fingers or fingers cut from sponge cake in fruit juice or sherry.

Whip cream and sweeten with sugar.

Arrange alternate rows of macaroons and whipped cream in a cut-glass dish.

Top with chocolate and let stand 2 hours in refrigerator before serving. (Serves 6.)

SABAYON SAUCE

4 egg yolks
2/3 cup sugar

1 cup white wine
1 tbsp. rum OR kirsch (optional)

Whip egg yolks and sugar together until mixture becomes light and lemon-coloured.

Stir in wine and put in top of double boiler with cold water in the bottom.

Cook, stirring constantly, until water comes to a boil or till mixture is thickened and creamy.

Add rum or kirsch.

Serve hot on soufflé, plum pudding or any other warm pudding.

The Canadian Harvest: Preserves and Pickles

Next to baking bread, I think pickling gives me the most satisfaction. Freezing I consider a chore, but making relishes, pickles, jams and preserves is fun. It also fills the house with fantastic aromas. And don't think you have to have a storage room in the basement before you can attempt this department of cooking. Even my friends in apartments make jams and pickles for giving away when storage space under the bed is filled.

ONE-DAY SWEET GHERKINS

2 qts. gherkins
1/2 cup salt
2 qts. water
6 cups brown sugar
1 qt. cider vinegar
1 tbsp. allspice

1 tbsp. whole cloves
1/2 tbsp. celery seed
1/2 tbsp. mustard seed
1 stick cinnamon
Bay leaves (optional)
Small hot red pepper (optional)

Wash gherkins and soak overnight in a brine made by combining salt and water.

Drain gherkins in the morning, rinse them in hot water and drain again.

Place brown sugar and vinegar in a preserving kettle and bring to a boil.

Add gherkins, then allspice, whole cloves, celery seed, mustard seed and cinnamon tied together in a cheesecloth bag.

Remove kettle from heat and allow gherkins to cool in pickling syrup.

Remove spice bag and pack pickles into pint jars. Add 1 bay leaf and 1 small hot red pepper to each jar if desired.

Heat syrup to boiling point and fill the jars to over-flowing. Seal. (Makes 5 pints.)

PICKLED CRABAPPLES

2 1/2 qts. crabapples
3 cups sugar
2 cups cider vinegar
2 cups water

1 tbsp. whole cloves
1 tbsp. whole allspice
3-inch stick of cinnamon

Leave the stems on the crabapples but cut out blossom end.

Combine sugar, vinegar, water and spices, tied in a bag, in a saucepan. Bring syrup to a boil and boil for 5 minutes.

Add prepared fruit a few at a time to boiling syrup and cook gently until it is partially tender but not soft (about 10 minutes).

Remove fruit from syrup as soon as it is cooked, and pack in hot sterilized jars.

Discard spice bag after all the fruit is cooked, fill the jars to overflowing with the spiced syrup, and seal at once.

WINTER CHUTNEY

1/2 lb. dried apricots	1 small hot red pepper, seeded
1/2 lb. pitted dates	1 tbsp. salt
2 lb. sour pitted red cherries	1/2 cup preserved ginger, chopped
fresh or canned, drained	1/2 cup honey
1 cup seedless raisins	1 cup brown sugar
2 cloves garlic	1 cup wine vinegar

Soak apricots in enough water to cover for 1 hour.

Drain and reserve the liquid.

Chop apricots with dates, cherries, raisins, garlic and hot pepper.

Add salt and ginger and mix well. Let mixture stand for 1 hour.

Add honey, sugar, 1 cup of reserved apricot liquid and vinegar.

Bring mixture to a boil and simmer for 45 minutes or until the chutney is very thick, stirring frequently.

Seal in hot, sterilized pint jars. (Makes 4 or 5 jars.)

Screw-top jars containing vinegar should have wax-paper under the lid so vinegar doesn't come in contact with the metal.

SUMMER FRUIT RELISH

4 pears	1 1/2 cups cider vinegar
4 peaches	2 tsp. salt
4 ripe tomatoes	1/4 tsp. cayenne pepper
1 onion	1/8 tsp. ground cinnamon
1 green pepper	1/8 tsp. ground cloves
1/2 cup sugar	

Wash and peel pears, peaches, tomatoes and onion.

Core pears, pit peaches and seed green pepper.

Put fruit and vegetables through medium blade of a food chopper.

Mix ground fruit and vegetables with remaining ingredients, bring to a boil and simmer for 1 1/2 hours or until relish is thick. Stir frequently.

Pour into hot jars and seal. (Makes 3 pints.)

MY BEST FRUIT CHILI

4 qts. ripe tomatoes, chopped and peeled (8 lb.) OR 3 qts canned tomatoes	5 cups medium onions (about 12), peeled and chopped
1 qt. peaches OR pears (about 6), unpared and chopped	1 1/4 cups seeded sweet red peppers chopped
3 cups apples (about 6), unpared and chopped	2 1/2 tbsp. salt
	7 tbsp. mixed pickling spice
	2 1/2 cups granulated sugar
4 cups cider vinegar	

Combine tomatoes, peaches or pears, apples, onions, red peppers and salt.

Cook, uncovered, for 1 1/2 hours or until reduced one half. Stir occasionally.

Add pickling spice in cheesecloth bag, sugar and vinegar.

Cook, uncovered, for 1 hour or until quite thick, stirring frequently. Remove bag.

Pour into clean, hot jars. (Makes 7 to 8 pints.)

PRIZE CHILI SAUCE

15 choice, red tomatoes (about 3 3/4 lb.)
3 pimientos (sweet red peppers, fresh or canned)
1 sweet green pepper
2 large white cooking onions
2 1/2 cups good cider vinegar
1 1/2 cups granulated sugar

3 tsp. salt
Spice bag of fine cheesecloth containing:
2 or 3 cinnamon sticks, broken up
8 cloves
1 tbsp. celery seed
4 peppercorns (whole black pepper)
2 or 3 dried small red peppers

Wash peppers and onions; cut open peppers and remove seeds and white portions.

Peel onions and cut up with peppers and grind in food chopper, using medium fine blade.

Prepare spice bag and place it and vinegar in a 6-quart preserving kettle, bring to the boil and boil slowly for 12 minutes. Remove bag and drain.

Pour boiling water over tomatoes and allow to stand 1 to 2 minutes. Drain well in colander. Skin and cut into small pieces.

Add tomatoes, minced peppers and onions, 1/2 cup of the sugar and salt to spiced vinegar. Boil rather slowly for 1 hour, stirring occasionally.

Add remaining sugar and boil rapidly, stirring often until thick.

Skim if necessary and seal in sterilized jars.

PINK AND GREEN PEPPER RELISH

12 red peppers, seeded
12 green peppers, seeded
12 onions, peeled

2 tbsp. salt
2 cups sugar
4 cups cider vinegar

Put vegetables through medium blade of a food chopper.

Pour boiling water over vegetables and let stand for 10 minutes. Drain.

Add salt, sugar and vinegar. Bring to a boil and simmer for 20 minutes.

Seal in hot jars. (Makes 6 pints.)

UNCOOKED CURRANT RELISH

1 cup dried currants, soaked and drained
1 cup grated orange peel

1 or 2 small sweet gherkins, cut very finely
French dressing

Combine currants, peel (6 to 9 oranges), gherkins.

Moisten with French dressing.

Place in a clean glass jar and let stand 12 hours before serving. (Makes about 2 1/2 cups.)

Note: This relish will keep for 3 weeks in the refrigerator.

CRANBERRY ORANGE RELISH

1 lb. cranberries
1 or 1 1/2 oranges

2 cups sugar

Grind the cranberries with the coarse blade of a food chopper.

Peel the orange. Trim off all the white part and remove the seeds. Put the rind and pulp through food chopper.

Mix orange with sugar and cranberries.

Allow to stand a few hours before serving. Serve with fowl or cold ham. (Makes 1 1/2 pints.)

Note: If you wish to keep this relish for future use, pour into glass jars and cover with paraffin.

BREAD AND BUTTER PICKLES

6 large cucumbers, sliced
4 onions, sliced
1/4 cup salt (coarse is preferable)
1 pt. white vinegar

3/4 cup sugar
1 tsp. celery seed
1 tsp. mustard seed

Let cucumbers, onions and salt stand one hour, then drain.

Heat vinegar, sugar, celery and mustard seed and cook for 3 minutes after sugar has dissolved.

Pack vegetables in jars, add hot vinegar mixture to overflow and seal immediately. Let cool and store. (Makes 4 pints.)

OLD-FASHIONED CUCUMBER CHUNKS

1 gallon cucumbers, cut in chunks
1 1/2 cups salt
1 gallon water
9 cups cider vinegar

5 cups sugar
3 cups water
2 tbsp. mixed pickling spices
1 tsp. powdered alum

Place cucumber in a stone jar or enamel kettle.

Dissolve salt in 1 gallon water and pour brine over cucumbers.

Place a weighted plate on the top to keep cucumbers submerged and let stand 36 hours.

Drain and pour 4 cups of vinegar over cucumbers. Add enough water to cover and bring to a boil.

Simmer for 10 minutes and drain.

Combine 2 cups of sugar with 3 cups of water and balance of vinegar.

Add mixed pickling spices, tied in a bag, and bring to a boil. Simmer for 10 minutes.

Discard spice bag and pour spiced vinegar over cucumbers. Allow to stand for 24 hours.

Drain liquid into a kettle and add balance of sugar and powdered alum.

Bring to a boil, pour over cucumbers, and let stand for 24 hours.

Pack pickles into hot jars. Bring syrup to a boil and pour it, while boiling hot, over the pickles until it covers them. Seal jars. (Makes 5 quarts.)

PICKLED CABBAGE

1 small cabbage, white or red   1 qt. white vinegar
1/4 cup salt   1 cup sugar
1/4 cup pickling spice

Shred cabbage medium fine and measure. (You should have 2 quarts.)

Sprinkle with salt and let stand 5 or 6 hours.

Tie pickling spice up in a cheesecloth bag.

Pour the vinegar and sugar into a saucepan and heat it to a bubbling boil. Turn down heat, drop in the spice bag and cook very gently, uncovered, for 15 to 20 minutes.

Rinse cabbage and dry it thoroughly.

Pack into sterilized pint jars, lift out the spice bag and pour vinegar mixture over cabbage.

Seal securely and store several weeks to develop flavour. (Makes about 4 pints.)

LAC ST. JEAN PICKLED BLUEBERRIES

1 pt. firm blueberries   1 tsp. vinegar
2 tbsp. molasses   1/2 cup brown sugar, well packed

Wash and pick over the blueberries.

Mix berries in the molasses and vinegar.

Place alternate layers of the blueberry-molasses-vinegar mixture and the brown sugar in an earthenware crock and store in a cool place. (Fills about 4 to 5 6-oz. jars.)

HORS-D'OEUVRE TURNIPS

1 qt. turnips, peeled and cut up   1 clove garlic, peeled
1 pt. vinegar   1 tsp. salt
1 red pepper pod   1 tbsp. mixed whole spices

Pack the turnips in a sterilized jar.

Mix the remaining ingredients and pour cold over the turnips. Seal and let stand for at least one month.

Chill thoroughly before serving. (Fills 4 to 5 6-oz. jars.)

UNCOOKED TOMATO RELISH

6 to 8 tomatoes, unpeeled	1 tsp. dry mustard
2 medium-sized green peppers	1/2 tsp. celery seed
2 medium-sized onions	1 tsp. basil OR savory
2 tsp. salt	1/4 cup cider, wine vinegar OR
1/4 cup salad oil	malt vinegar

Dice tomatoes, green peppers and onions. Mix together. Place in a colander and allow to drain for 20 minutes. Place in bowl.

Add salt, mustard, celery seed, basil or savory, vinegar and salad oil.

Taste for seasoning and add a little sugar if you prefer a sweeter relish.

UNCOOKED PEPPER RELISH

Salt	4 tbsp. sugar
1 medium-sized cabbage, finely	2 tbsp. celery seed
chopped	Vinegar
3 large green sweet peppers,	
finely chopped	

Sprinkle a small handful of salt over the cabbage and let stand for 40 minutes.

Squeeze between the hands to get out all the water.

Add peppers, sugar and celery seed and cover with vinegar.

Seal cold in sterilized jars. (Fills about 3 medium jars.)

SPICED TOMATO BUTTER

1/2 gal. tomatoes, seeds and skins	1 tsp. ground cinnamon
removed	1 tsp. allspice
1/2 gal. apples, peeled and diced	1 tsp. ginger
2 1/2 lb. brown sugar	1 tsp. cloves
1/2 pt. vinegar	

Mix all ingredients together. Bring to a good boil, then cook down slowly until the mixture is thick.

Seal in sterilized jars. (Makes about 4 to 5 quarts.)

MUSTARD MIX PICKLES

3 large cucumbers	White vinegar
1 qt. green tomatoes	1 oz. powdered turmeric
3 heads cauliflower	4 oz. ground mustard
3 red peppers	2 cups flour
3 green peppers	6 3/4 cups white sugar
2 qts. button onions	2 qts. cider vinegar
1 qt. small gherkins	1 qt. water

Brine: 1 cup coarse salt to 9 cups of water

Prepare vegetables as follows:

Cut unpeeled cucumbers in chunks or dice; cut tomatoes in 6 or 8 pieces; break cauliflower into flowerets; slice peppers in strips; peel small onions but leave gherkins whole.

Place each vegetable in a separate bowl when ready.

Cover all vegetables with a brine made from 1 part coarse salt to 9 parts cold water, and allow vegetables to stand overnight. (For this recipe, 1 cup salt to 9 cups water is sufficient. If recipe is doubled, proportions should also be doubled.)

In the morning, drain and cook each vegetable separately (using several pots) in salted water and vinegar, using 1 part vinegar to 2 parts water. (Add 1 tsp. coarse salt.)

Boil briskly until nearly tender — 5 to 10 minutes, depending on vegetables. Drain well.

Meanwhile, make a paste by blending the turmeric, mustard, flour and sugar, and adding cider vinegar and water and stirring until mixture is smooth. Then boil, stirring frequently, until mixture is smooth and creamy.

Combine all vegetables in large kettle and pour sauce on top. Bring to a boil and simmer 10 minutes.

Pour into hot, sterilized jars and seal. (Makes 10 to 12 quarts.)

OLD ENGLISH CHUTNEY

24 ripe tomatoes
12 peaches
4 onions
4 green peppers
1 cup preserved ginger in syrup

1/2 lb. seedless raisins
4 cups brown sugar
1 tbsp. salt
3 cups vinegar

Peel and chop tomatoes, peaches and onions.
Seed and chop peppers and ginger.
Combine ingredients in a preserving kettle. Bring to a
boil and cook slowly for 3 hours or until chutney is thick.
Stir frequently.
Seal in hot jars. (Makes 4 pints.)

PICKLED WATERMELON RIND

1 medium watermelon
1 gallon cold water
1 tbsp. powdered alum
10 cups sugar
6 cups cider vinegar

2 cups water
3 lemons, unpeeled and sliced thin
6 cinnamon sticks
2 tbsp. whole cloves
1/2 whole nutmeg

Peel and remove all the green and pink portions from
the rind of watermelon. Cut into long sticks or 1 x 1-inch
squares or circles. Soak overnight in 1 gallon cold water in
which powdered alum has been dissolved.
Drain, rinse and cover with fresh cold water (just enough
to cover) in the morning. Bring to a boil, cover and simmer
for 35 minutes.
Combine sugar, vinegar and 2 cups of water and boil
for 10 minutes.
Tie lemon slices, cinnamon sticks, whole cloves and
nutmeg in cheesecloth and add to syrup.
Drain watermelon and rinse again under cold water.
Add to hot syrup and cook until watermelon is slightly transparent. (Cooking time should be anywhere from 40 to 60
minutes, depending on the watermelon.)
Pack in hot jars and seal at once. (Makes 8 to 12 6-oz.
jars.)

PEPPERY ONION RELISH

14 medium-sized onions, very thinly sliced
6 green bell peppers, seeded and ground

3 to 6 long hot red peppers, ground OR 1 to 3 dried hot peppers
1 qt. white vinegar
3 cups sugar
2 tbsp. salt

Mix vegetables in a large bowl.

Cover with boiling water and let stand for 4 minutes. Drain well in a colander.

Return vegetables to the mixing bowl and cover again with boiling water.

Let stand for 4 minutes and then drain as before.

Put vinegar, sugar and salt in a kettle over low heat, stirring until sugar and salt are dissolved.

Add vegetables and bring to a boil.

Boil for 15 minutes. Seal in hot sterilized jars. (Makes about 6 pints.)

ADELE'S GRAND LAKE RELISH

1 qt. (6 large) cucumbers
10 large onions
1 large cauliflower
4 green peppers
Salt
7 cups brown sugar
1/2 gallon vinegar

1 tsp. turmeric
1 oz. celery seed
2 oz. mustard seed
2/3 cup flour
1/8 lb. dry mustard
Vinegar

Put cucumbers, onions, cauliflower and peppers through mincer separately. Place vegetables in separate bowls, add a handful of salt and cover with boiling water. Let stand overnight, then drain well and mix together.

Combine brown sugar, vinegar and turmeric in a large pot. Place celery seed and mustard seed in a small cotton bag and add to pot. Heat.

Mix flour and dry mustard with a little vinegar and add to syrup. Stir out all lumps, then add drained vegetables.

Cook slowly until thick. Seal in hot jars. (Makes 6 pints.)

HOT DOG RELISH

12 sweet green peppers, seeded
12 onions, peeled
12 green tomatoes
1/2 cup salt
4 cups cider vinegar

6 cups sugar
2 tsp. dry mustard
1 tsp. allspice
1/4 tsp. cayenne

Put vegetables through medium blade of a food chopper. Sprinkle with salt and let stand for 4 hours. (It is not necessary to peel the tomatoes before grinding unless the skins are particularly tough.)

Drain, rinse in clear water and drain again.

Combine vinegar and sugar in a kettle and bring liquid to a boil.

Add vegetables, mustard and spices. Boil for 10 minutes and seal in hot jars. (Makes 6 pints.)

SPICED GOOSEBERRIES

2 qts. gooseberries
4 1/2 cups brown sugar
1 cup cider vinegar
2-inch cinnamon stick

8 cloves
1/4 tsp. ground nutmeg
2 whole allspice
1/2 cup water

Wash gooseberries and cut off ends.

Combine sugar, vinegar and spices in an enamel pickling vessel, add water and boil for 5 minutes.

Add berries and simmer for 30 to 40 minutes.

When syrup is thick and berries are tender, pour into hot, sterilized jars and seal. Serve with roasts and stews and with curry dishes instead of chutney. (Makes approximately 8 6-oz. jars.)

In a year when rain is heavy, berries make a thinner jam than in the year of the dry spell.

SWEET AND SOUR PEPPER JAM

| 12 large red sweet peppers | 1 1/2 lb. sugar |
| 1 tbsp. salt | 2 cups vinegar |

Stem and seed peppers. Chop flesh finely.

Sprinkle with salt and allow to stand for 3 to 4 hours, then rinse in cold water.

Place peppers in a kettle with sugar and vinegar.

Bring to a boil and simmer until jam is thick, stirring frequently.

Pour into jars and seal. (Makes 6 6-oz. jars.)

RED PEPPER JAM

My son Joey's favourite jam which he eats with strong cheddar and scones.

12 large red sweet peppers	1/2 cup water
2 tbsp. coarse salt	1 lemon, quartered
1 1/2 cups cider vinegar	3 cups sugar

Wash and remove seeds from peppers. Pass through meat chopper and sprinkle with salt. Let stand 4 hours.

Drain well and add vinegar, water and lemon.

Simmer 30 minutes and remove lemon.   Add sugar.

Boil for about 1 hour until mixture has a jam consistency, stirring occasionally.

Pour into clean, hot sterilized jars and seal. (Makes 6 6-oz. jars.)

BITTER ORANGE MARMALADE

Cut 6 bitter oranges in half. Squeeze out juice and seeds and strain juice into preserving kettle.

Place seeds in a small bowl, and just cover them with warm water. Let stand overnight.

With kitchen scissors cut the orange peel into fine slivers along with any bits of pulp sticking to it.

Add peel to juice and weigh or measure.

Add 1 cup of water for each cup of juice and peel and let stand overnight. In the morning drain all jelly off the seeds into the juice and peel.

Keep spooning the liquid in the kettle over the seeds until no jelly remains on them, and they no longer feel slippery.

Bring the mixture in the kettle to a boil and simmer over low heat for 2 hours. (Do not boil as moisture will evaporate.)

Weigh again or measure, and to every pound of juice and peel add 1 pound of sugar or 1 cup of sugar to each cup of juice and peel.

Bring again to a boil and boil rapidly for 30 minutes to jelly point, or 220 degrees on a thermometer.

Pour into jelly jars and seal.

GRAPE CONSERVE

4 lb. Concord grapes	1 cup seedless raisins
1 orange	1/2 tsp. salt
4 cups sugar	1 cup walnuts, chopped

Skin grapes. Do not discard skins. Boil pulp 10 minutes stirring often. Strain through sieve.

Seed orange and grind whole orange coarsely.

Add orange pulp and any juice to grape pulp. Add sugar, raisins and salt.

Bring to a rapid boil, stirring constantly, and cook till mixture has thickened (about 10 minutes). Add grape skins.

Boil for 10 minutes, remove from heat, add nuts, pack and seal in sterilized jars. (Makes about 4 pints.)

Eat on toast or with any cold meat or fowl.

PINEAPPLE MINT JELLY

1 cup fresh mint, chopped
1/2 cup water
2 tbsp. sugar
2 cups unsweetened pineapple
  juice (canned)

1/2 cup lemon juice
4 cups sugar
1/2 bottle liquid pectin
Artificial green colouring

Cover mint with water and 2 tbsp. sugar. Let stand overnight and then strain.

Add pineapple juice, lemon juice and 4 cups sugar to this mint juice. Bring to a full rolling boil, stirring constantly.

Add pectin and boil hard for 30 seconds.

Add a little colouring, skim and pour into sterilized glasses. Seal at once with hot paraffin. (Makes about 6 6-oz. glasses.)

HERB JELLY

(The amount of parsley or other herbs used indicates how much of the other ingredients are necessary.)

Parsley (or see below) leaves
Sugar

Lemons OR limes
Gelatin

Pick the top tender leaves from sprigs of fresh parsley and wash well. Press the leaves down tightly in a saucepan and just cover with cold water. Bring to a boil and cook slowly until the leaves are tender.

Strain through a jelly bag, discard leaves and simmer juice until it is reduced about one third.

Add 3/4 cup sugar and the juice and rind of 1/2 lemon or lime to each cup of parsley extract.

Boil the mixture for 25 minutes.

Add 1 tsp. gelatin softened in a little cold water to each cup of hot syrup. Dissolve gelatin thoroughly.

Remove from heat and put into jelly glasses. Seal with paraffin. Parsley jelly is delicious served with meat or as an aspic with cream cheese. Fresh rosemary, thyme, basil or other herbs may also be made into jelly by using this recipe.

MINTED RASPBERRY JELLY

4 cups raspberry juice   1 8-oz. bottle pectin
7 1/2 cups granulated sugar   Mint leaves

Crush raspberries and extract juice through a jelly bag or large piece of cotton flannel or several layers of cheese cloth.

If berries do not have the tart taste you like, you may add 1/4 cup lemon juice just before adding pectin.

Bring sugar and 4 cups of juice to a boil and add pectin, stirring all the time. Bring again to a full rolling boil and boil hard for half a minute. Remove from heat and skim.

Pour right away into clean, sterilized jelly jars to within 1/2 inch of the top. Drop in a mint leaf and cover immediately with hot paraffin.

Cool and cover with sterilized tin covers or air-tight foil covers. (Fills about 10 6-oz. jars.)

Note: Jelly will be cloudy if the jelly bag is squeezed while juice is being extracted.

SWEET CIDER JELLY

1 qt. sweet apple cider   3 whole cloves
   OR apple juice   1 cup fruit pectin
7 1/2 cups sugar   1 tbsp. lemon juice
1 2-inch stick cinnamon

Place cider or apple juice, sugar, cinnamon and cloves in large saucepan and bring to a boil.

Stir in pectin and lemon juice and bring to a full rolling boil. Boil hard for 1 minute.

Remove from heat and let stand 1 minute.

Remove spices. Skim and pour quickly into sterilized dry glass jars.

Seal at once with paraffin. (Makes 3 pints.)

RED RASPBERRY AND CURRANT JELLY

4 1/2 cups (2 1/4 lb.) juice   1/2 bottle liquid fruit pectin
7 cups (3 lb.) sugar

Crush thoroughly about 1 1/2 lb. fully ripe currants. Add 1/2 cup water and bring to a boil.

Crush thoroughly about 1 1/2 qts. fully ripe raspberries. Do not cook.

Place fruit in jelly cloth and squeeze out juice.

Measure sugar and juice into large saucepan and mix. Bring to a boil over high heat, and add pectin at once, stirring constantly. Then bring to a full rolling boil and boil hard for 1 minute.

Remove from heat, skim, pour quickly into glasses and cover with paraffin. (Makes about 11 6-oz. glasses.)

FRESH GRAPE JELLY

3 lb. ripe grapes   7 cups (3 lb.) sugar
1/2 cup water   1/2 bottle fruit pectin

To prepare juice, stem grapes and crush thoroughly. (makes about 4 cups or 2 lb. juice)

Add water, bring to boil, cover and simmer for 10 minutes.

Place fruit in jelly cloth or bag. Squeeze out juice.

Measure sugar and juice into large saucepan and mix.

Bring to a boil immediately and add fruit pectin at once, stirring constantly.

Bring to a full rolling boil and boil hard for 1/2 minute.

Remove from fire, skim, pour quickly into sterilized jars. Seal with paraffin. (Makes about 10 6-oz. jars.)

MINT HONEY JELLY

3 cups strained honey   1/2 cup liquid commercial pectin
1 cup water   2 or 3 drops oil of mint
Juice of 1/2 lemon

Mix honey, water and lemon juice in a saucepan and heat quickly to a boiling point.

Add pectin and stir constantly. Bring syrup to a rolling boil and remove at once from the heat.

Add oil of mint, skim and pour into sterilized jelly glasses.

Seal with paraffin. This is a good dietetic jelly and the mint may be replaced by other flavours or omitted. (Makes 4 6-oz. jars.)

MINT JELLY

1 cup boiling apple juice   2 tbsp. mint extract
1 cup fresh mint leaves, firmly   3/4 cup sugar
  packed   Green food colouring

Pour boiling apple juice over mint leaves and let stand for 1 hour. Press juice from leaves.

Add mint extract and bring to a boil.

Add sugar and boil rapidly until it reaches the jelly stage.

Tint jelly with a few drops of green food colouring and pour into hot jelly glasses. (Makes 2 glasses.)

245

CUCUMBER MARMALADE

2 lb. cucumbers	1 box powdered fruit pectin
3 1/2 cups sugar	1/4 cup lemon juice
	1 to 2 tbsp. grated lemon rind

Peel cucumbers and chop finely or grind. Measure 2 1/2 cups into a large saucepan. Measure sugar and set aside. Place saucepan containing cucumber over high heat.

Add powdered fruit pectin, lemon juice and rind and stir until mixture comes to a hard boil. Stir in sugar at once, bring to a full rolling boil, and boil hard for 1 minute, stirring constantly.

Remove from heat, then stir and skim by turns for 5 minutes to cool slightly to prevent floating particles.

Ladle quickly into glasses and seal at once with paraffin. (Makes about 6 6-oz. glasses.)

If desired, a few drops of green colouring may be added while mixture is coming to a boil.

CARROT MARMALADE

4 cups raw carrots, chopped	1/2 tsp. ground cloves
3 cups sugar	1/2 tsp. ground allspice
Juice and grated rind of 2 lemons	1/2 tsp. ground cinnamon

Combine all ingredients and bring to a slow boil. Reduce heat, simmer, stirring constantly until thick.

Seal. You will find this excellent with meat or game. (Makes about 4 to 5 6-oz. jars.)

Tools and Utensils

THE REVOLUTIONARIES

Let's talk first about two developments in cooking equip-
ment that are going to revolutionize life in the kitchen.
They are the French-made food processor called Cuisinart
(Magi-Mix in France) and the microwave oven.

Cuisinart burst on the American scene more than a year
ago and it is now available in Canada. It is a joy to have
in the kitchen. It combines the functions of the electric
blender, the whisk, the food mill, the grater, meat grinder,
chef's knife, potato ricer and electric mixer. It does not
dice, whip cream or beat egg whites to full volume but it
makes sauces, soups, pâtés, even pastry and yeast dough
and does other jobs which experienced cooks may find
tricky or tedious. It doesn't occupy too much space on
the counter and is easy to empty and scrape out. A
notable advantage is that it doesn't have too many parts —
one steel cutting knife, a plastic knife which is rarely used,
and two discs for grating and slicing.

A microwave oven represents a major investment. Having
one in my kitchen has changed my attitude about preparing
meals on the run and it has removed the pressure which
goes along with being a working mother. The oven has a
defrost cycle so it's no longer a catastrophe if I forget to
take out a casserole from the freezer before leaving the

house. Imagine a baked potato ready in five minutes, a chicken casserole in 20, brownies in six, boiled milk in one — and, in addition to saving time, the oven uses 75 percent less energy than a conventional oven.

KNIVES

Good knives are the base of good cooking. It is a waste of money to buy cheap ones. Start with an 8" or 10" chef's chopping knife in either carbon or stainless steel. You'll also find a boning knife useful and efficient. It removes bone and inedible pieces from meat and it whittles off every last morsel from the Sunday roast. Next, a good 10" slicer (I don't like electric knives), a small paring knife and a steel to keep all of these sharp at all times. Knives should be sharpened before and after use.

POTS AND PANS

My most sincere advice is not to buy *sets* of anything. Choose your pots one by one and expect to pay a good price for them. In my opinion, a good pot is one you can pass on to your children in good condition. When I was married over 20 years ago, I bought for beauty's sake, and like many women my age have seen two or three brands of pots come and go from the kitchen. Today, I would advise anyone equipping a kitchen for the first or final time to buy at least one or two pieces of tin or silver-lined French copper. Copper is the most rewarding metal to cook in but it must be thick copper — 1/8" to be exact. Sauces cook smoothly in copper because it doesn't need high heat, distributes the heat evenly and allows for long, slow top-of-stove simmering which most pots don't permit. Next turn your attention to selecting Italian stainless steel pots which have a heavy aluminium exterior bottom. They are beautifully shaped, are heavy and balanced, and are ideal for sauce-making.

CASSEROLES

For casseroles that can go to the table from the oven, nothing surpasses enamel-covered ironware. In it, pot roast, stew or any dish which requires lengthy cooking does beautifully.

Since I first wrote this book, the clay pot has been reborn.
What I thought might be another passing fad has become a
basic utensil for many cooks. The unglazed pot is an oven
within your oven, leaves your oven clean, and roasts without
adding fat or liquid. You can even forget your clay pot in
the oven and though your supper may be overcooked, it won't
be ruined. It is best to cook at 400 degrees F. The meat
browns but remains moist. Kids can be taught to prepare
a satisfactory meal in the clay pot because there is no advance
preparation needed. But care must be taken to avoid breakage
in handling or washing — place the hot clay pot on a wooden
board or a dry dish towel, never on a cool counter or wet
surface.

FRYING PANS

The Canadian old-timer, the black cast iron model, is a must —
start frying in it. But you will need a number of frypans in
different metals for different jobs. A stainless steel pan with
aluminum bottom and a lid is great for all sautéeing jobs —
cutlets, liver, browning any meat and for reheating foods in a
hurry. An enamelled iron pan is also useful and so is an
electric frypan which is good for grilled cheese sandwiches,
French toast, pancakes and general cooking on boat trips,
cottage holidays and camping expeditions where an electrical
outlet is available.   For indoor barbecuing, the iron ridged
pan is excellent for steaks and hamburgers and there are new
French-made electric steak grills which do appetizing jobs on
meats and vegetables which you normally barbecue.

If you get into omelette-making, equip yourself with a pan
just for that. A wonderful non-stick surface builds up after
constant use which frequent washing would destroy so it's
best just to wipe out the pan with a paper towel after each
use. If you feel at times it needs more thorough cleaning,
heat some oil and rub coarse salt into it with a paper towel.
Wipe out with a clean paper towel till dry.   Omelette pans,
whether made in cast aluminum, spun aluminum, grey
iron, enamelled iron or lined with teflon or tefal, have one

thing in common: they are made with sloping sides so that the omelette can be rolled out neatly onto a plate. For crêpes, too, there's a special pan to be used for that one purpose. It is black iron and is used for turning out the crêpes which can then be flambéed in a copper crêpe pan over a small réchaud at table.

FISH PANS

If you eat a lot of fish, a fish poacher is a necessity. A poacher is a long, narrow vessel equipped with a rack to keep the fish intact. You can also use it for lobsters, clams, mussels, corn-on-the-cob and any vegetable you want to cook a lot of. Oval-shaped fish frying and au gratin pans are helpful because of their shape which permits fillets and whole small fish to cook with lots of fin-room. There is also a cast-iron fish grill pan, like the steak grill, which gives the same results as an out-door barbecue. But if you insist on cooking outdoors, you can buy a French fish grill made of wire and hinged like an old-fashioned campfire toaster. In France, the fish is sometimes grilled on a bed of fennel over the fire, set aflame with armagnac and finally has wet parsley thrown on it to douse the fire.

THE WOK

The Wok is China's all-purpose pan. It has deep, sloping sides and allows you to cook meat, fish and vegetables quickly over high heat. This is known as stir-fry, blitz or chow cooking.

SALAD DRIER

The salad drier beats 12 tea towels by a mile in drying out lettuce for a bowl of crisp greens. Dry lettuce holds the vinaigrette while wet lettuce lets it slide down to the bottom of the bowl. The Swiss salad rotor will also dry out parsley, herbs, spinach, strawberries — and potatoes before deep-frying.

Index

255